Of any book that Christine Caine has written, *Unashamed* has unmatched potential to bring deep healing into the lives of those who are broken and hurting. Each chapter is overflowing with raw transparency, healing grace, and scriptural hope. Whether you are struggling or know someone who is, this book will build your faith and equip you to move from shame to freedom and God's ultimate plan for your life.

–**Craig Groeschel,** senior pastor of Life.Church and author
of *#Struggles—Following Jesus in a Selfie-Centered World*

Christine Caine is undeniably anointed, unashamedly Christ-focused, and unguardedly real. Simply—her work is unparalleled. You—*your soul*—can't afford not to read her.

–**Ann Voskamp,** *New York Times* bestselling author
of *The Greatest Gift* and *One Thousand Gifts*

There's no one better equipped than my friend Christine Caine to speak to the power of shedding shame in the lives of believers. Her words here provide a pathway to freedom from a life shaped by shame. Her sincere and strong voice will inspire you, and her own display of courage will give you strength to step fully into God's love and grace.

–**Judah Smith,** lead pastor, The City Church, Seattle, and
New York Times bestselling author of *Jesus Is* _____.

I memorized the verse from Romans about there being no shame or condemnation for those of us who are in Christ Jesus when I was a little girl; unfortunately, I was still crippled by shame as a grown woman decades later. From my experience, shame is one of the most effective tools the enemy uses to oppress believers and emasculate the church. Which makes this book a MUST READ. Frankly, I encourage you to buy several cases of these puppies and pass them out to your entire community!

–**Lisa Harper,** author and Bible teacher

In *Unashamed*, Christine Caine acknowledges that shame does not discriminate—it seeps into the lives of the successful as well as the downcast. But Christine shares as only she can—with great passion and authenticity—about the path away from darkness and shame. A path to freedom. God is bigger than our pasts, bigger than our mistakes. If you let it, *Unashamed* will transform your life and set you on a path to the abundant life God has for you.

–**Mark Batterson,** *New York Times* bestselling author of *The Circle Maker* and lead pastor of National Community Church

Shame holds us back, holds us down, and holds us hostage. But in *Unashamed*, Christine shows us we don't have to let this be the reality of our lives. Her raw honesty and unwavering belief in God's good plan is the refreshing encouragement your soul needs!

–**Lysa TerKeurst,** *New York Times* bestselling author and president of Proverbs 31 Ministries

If the enemy's weapons of choice are shame and fear, then think of *Unashamed* as a heavenly atomic bomb.

–**Steven Furtick,** pastor, Elevation Church, and *New York Times* bestselling author

UNASHAMED

DROP THE BAGGAGE, PICK UP YOUR
FREEDOM, FULFILL YOUR DESTINY

CHRISTINE CAINE

ZONDERVAN

Unashamed
Copyright © 2016 by Christine Caine

Requests for information should be addressed to:
Zondervan, 3900 *Sparks Dr. SE, Grand Rapids, Michigan 49546*

ISBN 978-0-310-34073-7 (audio)

ISBN 978-0-310-34072-0 (ebook)

Library of Congress Cataloging-in-Publication Data

Names: Caine, Christine, author.
Title: Unashamed : drop the baggage, pick up your freedom, fulfill your destiny /
    Christine Caine.
Description: Grand Rapids : Zondervan, 2016.
Identifiers: LCCN 2015049864 | ISBN 9780310340706 (hardcover)
Subjects: LCSH: Christian women — Religious life. | Liberty — Religious
    aspects — Christianity. | Shame — Religious aspects — Christianity. | Self-
    realization — Religious aspects — Christianity.
Classification: LCC BV4527 .C24 2016 | DDC 248.8/43 — dc23 LC record available at
    http://lccn.loc.gov/2015049864

Published in association with the literary agency of David O. Middlebrook, 4501
Merlot Avenue, Grapevine, Texas 76051

Cover design: Jessica Davis
Cover photography: David Dobson Photography
Interior design: Kait Lamphere

First Printing March 2016 / Printed in the United States of America

To my beloved friend, Beth Moore.

"Each friend represents a world in us,
a world not born until they arrive,
and it is only by this meeting that a new world is born."
—Anais Nin

I will be forever grateful that our worlds collided.
Your friendship is a priceless gift.

Therefore have I set my face like flint,
and I know I will not be put to shame.

—Isaiah 50:7

CONTENTS

INTRODUCTION

I spent the first twenty-two years of my life shackled by shame. Looking back, I realize I had always felt it. It had been a part of my life from my earliest memories.

I felt it when I was rejected. Made to feel unworthy. Of no value.

I felt it when I was abused. And couldn't tell anyone. And believed it was somehow my fault.

I felt it when I tried to hide who I was, apologize for who I was, minimize my talents, or overachieve and compensate for feeling somehow "less than."

Have you felt it? If you're human, you have—and the result is always the same.

Shame makes us feel small. Flawed. Not good enough. And controlled.

Shame is the fear of being unworthy, and it adversely affects our relationship with God, ourselves, and others. It greatly hinders our ability to receive God's unconditional love—and share it with others.

Because of God's great love, I began to discover the power of God's Word to break through the lies I had believed—and to reveal the truth of who I am and why I was created. Notice that the key word in that sentence is *began*. Breaking free from the shackles of shame is not an overnight experience or a quick-fix, ten-step process. It is, however, a grand, ongoing adventure of discovering the depths of God's love and the huge scope of God's power to transform us, re-create us, and continually renew us. I am *still* discovering deeper aspects of those things, after all this time, and I know the process will not end until I meet him face to face. I wouldn't have it any other way. In fact, writing this book has been one more step on that journey for me, because shame loses its power when it is expressed. I hope that by sharing with you my story, you will open up your heart and allow God to lift the shame off you so you can flourish and become all that he's created you to be.

Do you struggle with the fear that you are not enough?

Are you afraid to let your true self be seen and known?

Are you always trying to gain approval? Trying to prove you are valuable and worthy to be loved?

Do you want to break the power of shame in your life?

Then join me through the pages of *Unashamed* to take your first steps in dropping the baggage of shame, picking up your freedom in Christ, and stepping into the fullness of the destiny—the shame-free life—God has in store for you.

I pray that this book helps you take the next steps on your journey to freedom and equips you to *keep* taking the next step. As you read, the enemy will be trembling, because he knows that once God has broken the chains of our slavery to shame, there will be no holding us back! So many of the things I'm experiencing now I never could have experienced if I'd remained a woman in hiding, ruled by shame. God has been writing a great story in my life—of his power to invade and transform a shamed woman into a beloved daughter, a treasured vessel of his Holy Spirit, a vital member of his body at work in this hurting world.

He wants to do the same for you. God created you for a unique purpose; he has a specific plan for your life; and he has a powerful destiny he wants you to fulfill. And guess what? Shame has no place in that purpose, plan, and destiny. Jesus came to set you free from shame . . .

> *It is for freedom that Christ has set us free. Stand firm, then, and do not let yourselves be burdened again by a yoke of slavery.*
>
> Galatians 5:1

Thank you for joining me as I share my journey from a shame-filled to a shame-free life. My heartfelt prayer is that you too will discover the power of a life lived free. It's the life God originally created you for, the life Jesus died to give you, the life you are worthy to live.

> *"The thief comes only to steal and kill and destroy; I have come that they may have life, and have it to the full."*
>
> John 10:10

> *With much love,*
> *Christine*

Chapter 1

SCHOOLED
IN SHAME

I've got your lunchbox packed, Christine," my mom called from the kitchen. "Come let me braid your hair."

I looked down at my brand-new shiny black shoes, checked that my white socks were evenly folded at my ankles, and skipped from my bedroom to collect the pretty bright pink lunchbox I'd been allowed to pick out for my first day of kindergarten. I had tried to eat a little breakfast that morning but couldn't manage more than a few bites. No problem. Who wanted to waste time on breakfast? The big day had finally arrived—my first day of school. I couldn't wait to get there! I fidgeted impatiently as my mom neatly braided my long, light brown hair into pigtails; then I bounded out of the house, pigtails flying, for the walk to school in the footsteps of my second-grade brother.

For some children, entering kindergarten is an exciting adventure of new friends, new songs and games, and new discoveries, while for others it can be a frightening separation from parents and the familiar security of home. I was definitely in the first category, an eager six-year-old filled with great expectations of good things.

I vividly recall taking my seat in the classroom for the first time and wiggling with excitement over the eye-widening, colorful world of bookshelves and chalkboards—a wonderland I was bursting to explore. But what excited me most was all the other children—a whole roomful of new playmates my own age! Until now, I'd seldom played with neighborhood children, though I had longed to. My play-mates had mostly been my brothers or my cousins at family gatherings. So I couldn't wait until outdoor lunch and recess when I could begin to make new friends.

Finally lunchtime came, and we all carried our lunch-boxes outside and sat on the asphalt playground. But this is where my warm waves of nostalgic memories give way to a scene that made my cheeks burn red and my heart sting.

I chose a spot next to a few other girls and unlatched my lunchbox, happy to find that my mom had packed my usual lunch—a feta cheese-and-olive sandwich. I was enjoying my first bite when Wayne, a boy sitting nearby, wrinkled his nose and cried out, "Phew! What's that awful smell? What's that stinky stuff you're eating?"

Suddenly, all eyes turned to me. Wayne's friend, Raymond, announced to all, "She's eating that Greek cheese." Then he eyed me suspiciously and asked, "Why can't you wogs eat normal food like everybody else? No wonder you all stink like garlic."

For a moment I froze; then my heart started to pound. I felt my face growing hot. The word he'd called me was a terrible word, a nasty word, an inflammatory racial slur for Greeks never used in my house, though I'd heard it before— spewed angrily by strangers in public places. Why was he calling me this? And my sandwich smelled normal to me, not stinky. Didn't everybody eat feta cheese?

I looked around hoping to see someone else with a lunch like mine, only to discover that all the other kids had something we never ate at my house—white-bread sandwiches spread with Vegemite, a distinctly Australian food paste. I felt exposed, an oddity on display, checked out by the puzzled and scowling faces of those who, only moments before, I had assumed were my new playmates.

I wanted to disappear.

Wayne and Raymond, on the other hand, bolstered by the attention of their newfound audience, grew bolder. "My dad says you people should go back to your own country. You don't belong here."

My stomach clenched. I didn't understand what he meant. Go back where? This *was* my country, wasn't it? I'd been born here in Australia. I'd lived on the same street my whole life. Didn't everyone else at lunch that day all live in the same Australian neighborhood my family did—Lalor Park? Why was he saying I didn't belong?

I looked at the other girls sitting alongside me, hoping to find a compassionate expression or reassuring sign, but every one of them looked away, pretending to ignore me. No one was going to come to my defense. I was all alone.

More stinging words about my heritage followed, accompanied by snickers from some of the other kids. I sat in silence, eyes to the ground, until Wayne and Raymond finally tired of taunting me and turned away. Obviously there was something wrong with me—something embarrassing about being Greek. No one else was mocked because of his or her food or family. I was, for reasons I did not understand, strange, different, and unpleasant to them, someone to be avoided.

Though my empty stomach rumbled, I'd lost my appetite. I stuffed my uneaten sandwich back into the lunchbox—the pretty pink lunchbox I'd been so excited about earlier—and snapped it shut. The minutes ticked by slowly. I watched longingly as others gathered in little groups and talked and played. But no one spoke to me. I sat quiet and alone, wanting to join in but feeling unwelcome, like an outsider.

Relief washed over me when the bell finally rang. On the way back to the classroom, fighting back tears, I secretly pulled my sandwich from my lunchbox and tossed it into the trash can. I never again wanted to be ridiculed for being different. I would try to be like everyone else. I didn't want to be Greek. Was I different in other ways I didn't realize? Did I have an accent? Did I use different words? Was there anything else about me that would make people laugh? From then on, I would try to not say or do anything that the others didn't.

The six-year-old me didn't really have a word that expressed what I felt that day. Since then, I've learned one.

Ashamed.

Almost every day for the rest of the year, no matter how hungry I was, I quietly carried the lunch my mom had lovingly packed for me over to the trash can and tossed it out.

Shame does that. It prompts us to toss away the good gifts we are given.

Lessons Learned

All I Really Need to Know I Learned in Kindergarten is the title of a famous book by Robert Fulghum. What he meant, of course, is that kindergarten is where we were taught what is expected of us to get along in this world. Share everything. Play fair. Hold hands and stick together. But the lesson I learned in kindergarten that day was the lesson of shame. I learned it so well in kindergarten that, by first grade, I'd come to expect the daily taunts and jeers, the name-calling and bullying. I'd also caught on to the fact that the hateful graffiti spray-painted on the walls of our housing projects was directed at my Greek immigrant family and me— the only Greeks in our low-income government housing neighborhood. I had learned through bitter experience that I could do nothing to erase the chasm between my classmates and me. My kindergarten plan to try to blend in had been met with failure. Instead, I was repeatedly shamed for the Greek blood running through my veins.

My response? I became a rough-and-tumble kid, ready to fight back. If I couldn't find security in my heritage, I would find it in strength and tenacity. If I couldn't win my classmates' affections and friendship, then I'd try to win their respect. Because I loved sports, especially soccer, I worked hard to be the best. I pushed myself to run the fastest, kick the hardest, set my sights on the best player—who was always a boy—and then work to outplay him. Soon, I more than held my own on the playground, competing evenly against the boys.

One day that year, now seven years old, as I walked home from school with my brother, a group of nine-year-old boys started pushing him. He tried to ignore them and continue toward home, but one of them yelled, "Come on, wog, too afraid to fight back?"

When the pushing escalated to punching, I'd had enough. Even though I was far smaller, I jumped to my brother's defense, leaping onto the back of one of the bigger boys and pulling his hair until he broke free and ran away. The others followed him, turning back occasionally to yell insults and call us names.

"I don't care what they say," I spat. "They'll think twice before they jump us again." But I *did* care. I cared a lot. I just wouldn't show it. Hiding my feelings had already become a way of life for me.

Shame does that. It teaches us to hide ourselves, to hunker down wherever we can find a wall of protection.

Despite the prejudice that surrounded me, I loved school and excelled at it. Books became my best friends, and my appetite for learning kept me eager for each new challenge. I was determined to prove to the world that I *was* worth something. Achievement, performance, accomplishment, success—these had become my means of seeking acceptance and approval. When the teacher asked questions, my hand shot up, and when assignments were given, I completed them without fail.

By second grade, I was emerging as a leader in the class, which I assumed was a good thing. I noticed that when we divided into groups, others often followed my lead. If a question stumped my classmates, their eyes, even the teacher's, often turned to me for the answer. When choosing up teams, academically or for sports, I was often among the first to be chosen. I assumed it wasn't because they liked me—I was still "that Greek girl"—but because they wanted to win.

Halfway through the year, report card day arrived. I was so excited to open the sealed envelope that I couldn't bring myself to wait—so as I walked down the road toward home, I tore it open to see what marks my teacher, Mrs. Black, had given me. My heart swelled with a sense of achievement as, scanning the page, I saw one high mark after another.

And then my eyes stopped at the bottom, locked on Mrs. Black's careful printing: "Christine is an excellent student but has to learn that she can't always be the leader."

My heart lurched. I felt as if I'd been punched in the stomach. Leading, whether through example or bossiness or just being the loudest, was the one place I had found for myself in second-grade society. Maybe I couldn't get them to like me, but I was actually quite good at getting them to follow me. And wasn't being a leader supposed to be a good thing? Something to be praised? Yet here I was, being chastised for the very thing I thought I was excelling in! I *wanted* to lead. I wanted to be something other than a poor and hated minority. I wanted to be strong. By working up the courage to step forward, to stand alone if need be, to be the leader, I'd discovered I had enough strength and skill that others wanted to follow me—even admire me. Me! The unwelcome Greek girl! But rather than encouraging and rewarding my leadership abilities, Mrs. Black was telling me to stop.

The joy I'd felt moments before morphed into embarrassment and hurt. While I'd thought that I was finding my place and proving my worth, had I all along been just a disappointment to my teacher, failing without even knowing it? Deflated, I slid the report card back into the darkness of the envelope.

Looking back at the teacher's words now, I realize that perhaps she saw a need to smooth the rough edges off a girl who was trying too hard, who may have been bossy or pushy or abrasive, and who tended to take over rather than work together with others. Today, I can give her the benefit of the doubt—maybe she was looking for ways to help me grow in social skills. But those thoughts were beyond the scope of my shamed second-grade heart. All I understood was that my teacher wanted me to stop being a leader, to stop being—or so it appeared to me—the best I could be.

Sadly, the final report card at the end of that year showed the results. Right next to her earlier comment, Mrs. Black had written: "Christine has settled down very well."

Yes, I'd gotten the message. Squelch my gifts of leadership. Stifle my strengths. Become more invisible. Be less than myself.

Shame does that. It pushes you down and prevents you from becoming all you could be.

Shame was my companion from my earliest memories, a huge part of my life and identity. And not just in school. Outside my home, my ethnic heritage was a reason for shame, but inside my home, I had almost the opposite problem: It seemed that I did not fit as I should into my culture or my gender. The messages of disapproval I perceived added fuel to the fire of shame that burned inside me. Since sports and books were my favorite pastimes, I threw myself into both with a passion, energized to be one of the best, the smartest, the fastest, the toughest. The only problem with that was—well—good little Greek girls weren't *supposed* to love sports and books!

"Christine, why can't you be like other girls? Why don't you play with dolls instead of spending so much time reading? That can't be healthy."

"Christine, stop playing ball with the boys. You should be in the kitchen, learning to cook."

"Why do you spend so much time on schoolwork? Boys don't like girls smarter than they are."

The message was loud and clear: A good Greek girl should want to learn to cook and play with dolls because her real purpose, her ultimate future, was to grow up, get married, and have babies. Any passions beyond those, the messages I heard at home clearly implied, were shameful.

My mom, wanting the best for my future and doing her best to motivate me in "girl" interests, signed me up for ballet lessons, which I hated. And when I complained, she would ask, "Christine, why do you like soccer more than ballet? What's wrong with you?"

You should have heard her the day she discovered that each time she dropped me off for ballet, I'd wait for her to drive away, drop my tutu to the ground, and tear off running to the soccer field to play with the boys. She flipped!

I don't recall a time in my life when I didn't feel that there was something wrong with who I was, something deficient in me. My sources of shame, however, went far beyond the ethnic prejudices of my schoolmates, the misdirected messages of my teacher, and the cultural pressures and expectations of my Greek family. What my mom and dad, teachers, and classmates didn't know was that I carried a shameful secret.

From my earliest memories, I was the victim of sexual abuse. Far too young to comprehend what was happening, I only knew that what was being done to me felt ugly and wrong, and it left me feeling that *I* was ugly and wrong. My parents did not know it was happening. These secret acts took place behind closed doors, and I had no words to describe them even if I had felt safe enough to try. But shame took hold from the very beginning, so I wouldn't have dared utter a word.

When you are abused, at first you are ashamed of what is happening to you. Over time, though, you begin to think it is *because of you* that it is happening. The abuse continued for years—throughout my entire childhood. It was hidden; it had always been hidden; and I believed it needed to stay hidden. After all, I thought, there must be something very wrong with me. *I must be at fault. I must be a bad person. I am not worth protecting. God must not love me. I guess I'm not worth his attention.*

Shame does that. It whispers lies to your soul.

Shackled by Shame

Shame is a powerfully painful emotion. Though as a child I lacked the understanding or vocabulary to define it, I knew well the many feelings of shame: humiliation, disgrace, unworthiness, embarrassment, anger, dishonor, remorse, anguish, sorrow, and self-reproach. I had no concept of the difference between the shame of what was being done to me and the shame of my own actions—they were inexplicably meshed into a mass of inner pain. I remember my face heated and my stomach churning. I remember wanting to duck down and disappear, to shrink down into myself where no one could see the ugly feelings of wrongness deep inside. And when I did dare step into the spotlight, to take the lead in something and excel, I worked hard to be sure that all those frightening feelings were locked away and invisible, so that no one would know they lurked within. I was a child damaged by shame, shackled to it, and I dragged it with me from childhood into adolescence and then into adulthood.

Most likely, you have done the same.

Experience and observation have shown me that countless women of all ages, on every continent, have been schooled in and shackled by shame. As I travel the globe, I meet thousands in my speaking engagements who are struggling and debilitated by shame. I see shame everywhere I look, including the church. It creeps into the heart, growing in shadowy places, until those struggling with it are too shamed to seek help from the very shame that enslaves them.

Shame lives within women who worship beside you at church, work in the next cubicle, attend your workout class, entertain you on TV, smile at you from magazine covers, or live next door. I've seen it in so many faces I've come to know.

I see shame in Emma, my friend Carol's granddaughter who saw her parents fight and do terrible things. She didn't know who was responsible for what. All she knew for sure was that she felt a terrible wrongness that made her want to hide. Little Emma, a child who had done nothing wrong.

Dianne was an honors student who dreamed of college. But her dad said he wouldn't waste money on a girl attending college. So she put herself through school. Once in her career, in a rewarding position, she was treated differently than her coworkers—because she was a woman.

Yun, a young Vietnamese girl, was forced to become a sex slave. Her repeated attempts to escape that life resulted in vicious beatings, one of which brought her to the attention not only of government social agencies but also of A21, a global ministry my husband, Nick, and I began in order to assist victims of human trafficking. Even under A21's protection, Yun continued to experience debilitating shame that almost defeated our attempts to help her find the life she wanted.

Shame compounded my friend Heather's lifelong struggle with mental illness that left her in a cell in a mental institution after a grisly suicide attempt—alone, disheveled, missing a shoe, covered in blood and vomit and urine. What she felt was not just fear and humiliation but shame.

Natalie was forever asked when she would marry. A successful lawyer, she had pursued her childhood dream, but everyone only cared if she was married or not. She came from a culture where everyone thought getting married was more important than having a life or a career. Those achievements were secondary. Every family gathering was another date with shame.

And there are women in the Bible who were made to feel shame. The woman with the issue of blood had been in hiding for twelve years when she touched the hem of Jesus' garment and was healed (Mark 5:25–34). She had been forced to live in shame as an outcast in her family and community, hidden away from everyone—all because of a condition she couldn't control.

The woman caught in adultery was literally drug out of bed and brought before Jesus (John 8:4–11). Her reputation sullied. Humiliated. Shamed. Judged. Rejected. Labeled.

Me. Emma. Dianne. Yun. Heather. Natalie.

The woman with the issue of blood and the woman caught in adultery.

Modern times. Biblical times.

We are just a few who represent the many stories I hear

every day about the kinds of experiences that produce and bind women with shame.

We have all been affected. But we can all be free.

Silent No More

Talking about my past and my struggle with shame used to be very difficult for me. I remember, in my early years of ministry, contending with shame's lies. *Others will find out you are weak,* shame whispered. *Then you will lose their respect and damage your ministry. Shhh. Hide. Don't be vulnerable! Project only strength.*

Oh yes! Shame lies. Big time. Even today, every now and then, unless I am vigilant, shame still tries to sneak up on me at the most unexpected times. The devil still lies to me, as he did back then. And he would love for me to believe his lies and remain silent rather than choosing to dig deeper, to root out more of his lies and shame in my life, and to encourage others to do the same.

But I cannot be silent.

Chapter 2

THE POWER OF SHAME

"Twenty-eight, twenty-nine, thirty. Ready or not, here I come!" And so begins the familiar game of hide and seek. My girls, Catherine and Sophia, at ten and fourteen, still enjoy it with their friends Parker and Ryan—though over the years their hiding skills have become far craftier. (Craftier, let's say, than the time a very young Sophia tried to hide in the clothes dryer but couldn't quite get her whole leg in. It's a dead giveaway when the dryer has a leg sticking out.) And their seeking skills have grown far more strategic and methodical.

My friend Carol recently told me a hide-and-seek story that paints a picture of innocence and trust—and reveals the work of shame. Carol's granddaughter, Emma, was two when first learning to play hide and seek. She would run to Carol, a twinkle in her eye, and say, "Grandma, play hide and seek. I hide. You find me." She announced their assigned roles every time, as if there were some doubt as to who would do the hiding and who would do the seeking. Emma always did the hiding.

Carol would close her eyes and begin a dramatic, slow countdown. She could hear Emma's giggles as she scurried to her favorite hiding place. Every time, no matter what room she started in, Emma went to the exact same hiding spot—behind Carol's big upholstered living room chair. Carol would announce her efforts as she did her searching: "Hmm. Where could Emma be? Is she in the closet? No. She's not in there. Is she under this blanket on the couch? No. Not there."

Meanwhile, giggles floated across the room from Emma's hiding place. Carol moved in closer and closer, until finally, when very close, she'd say, "Hmm. I wonder . . . could she be behind my big blue chair?"

At this point Emma would become very quiet, crouch down low, and—the most adorable thing of all—close her eyes! Surely, if she couldn't see Grandma, Grandma couldn't see her. Then Carol would pounce. "There you are! I found you!" She'd engulf her granddaughter in a hug and tickle her as she squealed with delight, then cuddle her until the inevitable . . .

"Again! Let's play again. I hide. You find me." And back to the same hiding place she'd go.

Oh, the naiveté of little Emma, choosing the same spot time and time again, giving away her location with wiggles and giggles, crouched down with eyes squeezed tightly shut, thinking Grandma couldn't see her. And the beauty of her anticipation awaiting the wonderful embrace of being found.

When I Learned to Hide

But for those of us schooled in shame, being found is no laughing matter. It is feared, not joyfully anticipated. Hiding is our go-to coping skill to guard ourselves against the pain of disapproval or judgment, condemnation or mockery, belittlement or exposure, or worse—just fill in the blank with your unique circumstance. We put on masks of pretense; we erect protective shields around our hearts to deflect the shame or distract unwanted attention. Enough practice and we become masters at hiding from others and eventually ourselves—and ultimately we hide from God, thinking that somehow, if we're not seeing him, then he must not be seeing us.

My hiding reflex took root as a young victim of sexual abuse, but as my childhood faded into adolescence, my shame did not fade with it—it intensified. I carried the weight of that secret throughout my teenage years and into my twenties. I had no recollection of ever being unashamed, of ever feeling free of guilt and a sense of wrongness—and so, since the thought of speaking it aloud was unbearable, I continued to hide those events and feelings from everyone I knew, confiding in absolutely no one.

Meanwhile, though the shaming messages I received at home about traditional Greek gender roles evolved as I grew older, their essence remained the same: "Christine, get your head out of those books and spend more time in the kitchen. Besides, a girl can't be more educated than the boys. No boy will want to marry you if you are too smart or too strong."

I got the message: Bringing home top grades would be met not with praise but with concern and disapproval. On the flip side, because academic and sport accolades were my primary sources of praise at school, and I so craved affirmation, I would not, could not, relinquish my achievements at school. I felt caught in a no-win scenario.

I will never forget the day when it occurred to me how to succeed at high school while hiding it from my family. It was report card day, and I was walking home, hungrily reading and rereading every positive mark, thrilled with all my 1s—the top grade one could earn, equivalent to an "A" in American schools. But despite my private satisfaction, I didn't want to face the condemnation of my mother for being "too smart." And then I had an idea. I pulled out my pen and carefully changed my 1s to 4s. It worked. My mom was satisfied that, finally, I wasn't too smart to catch the eye of some boy who might want to marry me. Her relief was visible! Mission accomplished.

I didn't like it. Knowing that I was being deceptive left me feeling guilty, which amplified my feelings of being unworthy of love. But I saw no other way. Wasn't I unworthy anyway? I believed so. So I, the hider, became even better at hiding. I worked to push my deception out of my mind—in essence, hiding it from myself—and I certainly wouldn't have dreamed of discussing it with God. The image of God I grew up with was not someone to whom you would actually pour out your heart. And as I'd learned from being abused, some things are simply better left unspoken.

We Weren't the First to Hide

Learning to hide may have been a new defense mechanism for me but not for humankind. I wasn't doing anything new that people hadn't been doing for centuries—well, actually, since the beginning of time. Hiding because of shame goes all the way back to the garden of Eden. But creation didn't start out that way. *"So God created mankind in his own image, in the image of God he created them; male and female he created them. God blessed them"* (Genesis 1:27–28).

You and I were created to reflect God's image. Do you know what that makes you and me? Not shame-bearers, but image-bearers of God himself. We were not designed to bear shame.

The story of the garden goes on to explain that when God designed Eden, he did so for our pleasure and our good, like everything else he gives us. *"The Lord God made all kinds of trees grow out of the ground—trees that were pleasing to the eye and good for food. In the middle of the garden were the tree of life and the tree of the knowledge of good and evil"* (Genesis 2:9).

But he did have just one simple rule in the garden: *"And the Lord God commanded the man, 'You are free to eat from any tree in the garden; but you must not eat from the tree of the knowledge of good and evil, for when you eat from it you will certainly die'"* (Genesis 2:16–17).

You're probably familiar with this story so far, but consider this very important verse: *"Adam and his wife were both naked, and they felt no shame"* (Genesis 2:25).

Why did God mention that Adam and Eve felt no shame? He must have had a reason; after all, he had options. He could have said that they felt no anxiety or pain or suffering. He could have instead told us what they *did* feel. "Adam and his wife were both naked, and they felt love." Or joy, or peace, or gratitude. But what he said was that they were naked and *felt no shame.*

I wonder if he did so because he knew that shame would be one of the enemy's most damaging weapons against us, and therefore God wanted us to know that, from the very beginning, shame was not his plan for us—that the perfect state for humankind is a shame-free life.

The Hebrew word for *shame* in this verse is stronger than "to be embarrassed." It is *bosh,* which literally means to be "utterly dejected" and to be "ashamed in front of one another."[1] It contains a sense of fear of exploitation or of evil. Before they ate from the fruit of the tree, Adam and Eve had no fear of evil—and that is how God created us to be.

You know what comes next. The serpent lies to the woman. The woman eats the forbidden fruit. The man does the same. And then the saddest thing happens. *"Then the eyes of both of them were opened, and they realized they were naked"* (Genesis 3:7).

And that is when shame invaded the world. Imagine what it must have been like as those first horrible feelings swept over them. Think of several of your own most shameful moments all wrapped into one moment of time. Remember that instinct to close your eyes, hide your face, and shrink, wishing you could just disappear. What was their response?

"They sewed fig leaves together and made coverings for themselves" (Genesis 3:7).

They covered themselves. Even before God showed up for a visit in the garden, they hid a part of themselves. Something had broken, and they knew it. They covered themselves with inadequate means—fig leaves. They went from total vulnerability and openness to hiding their bodies from each other. Separation, isolation, and division invaded their relationship in a heartbeat.

But they did more than hide their bodies from each other. They hid from God.

"Then the man and his wife heard the sound of the LORD God as he was walking in the garden in the cool of the day, and they hid from the LORD God among the trees of the garden" (Genesis 3:8).

The innocence and transparency between God and the man and woman he created had been tarnished. Adam and Eve, who had never known shame, were now ashamed and afraid. So they hid.

Separating Guilt from Shame

They acted just like little Emma "hiding" from her grandma behind the chair. Did they really think they could hide from God, that he didn't know exactly where they were, that he couldn't see them?

Now comes the very first recorded dialogue between God and the humans he created.

But the Lord God called to the man, "Where are you?"

He answered, "I heard you in the garden, and I was afraid because I was naked; so I hid."

And he said, "Who told you that you were naked? Have you eaten from the tree that I commanded you not to eat from?"

The man said, "The woman you put here with me— she gave me some fruit from the tree, and I ate it."

Then the Lord God said to the woman, "What is this you have done?"

The woman said, "The serpent deceived me, and I ate."

Genesis 3:9–13

What does it say about humankind that our very first recorded dialogue with God contains words of fear, hiding, and blame? It says that when sin entered the world, we immediately had a sinful, broken response to one another and to God.

Notice this: In those first few lines, Adam and Eve admit to fear and hiding. But they don't admit *guilt*. They don't admit responsibility for disobedience, only the consequences and causes of that disobedience. They could have spoken the plain, unvarnished truth: "We were hiding because you told us not to eat the fruit, and we disobeyed you and ate it anyway." But rather than confess what they did (guilt), they tried to hide who they were (shame), and in their shame, they resorted to blame.

Guilt and *shame* seem similar in meaning, but there is a significant difference. One rich resource that has fascinated me is the writing of Brené Brown, Ph.D., the author of *Women and Shame*. In an interview with *The Mothers Movement Online,* Brown defines shame as, "The intensely painful feeling or experience of believing we are flawed and therefore unworthy of acceptance and belonging." Contrast that with how she describes guilt:

> Guilt says: "You've done something bad," or "You've made a bad choice."
>
> Shame says: "You are bad."
>
> There is a big difference between "you made a mistake" and "you are a mistake."[2]

I put it this way: Guilt is about my *do*. Shame is about my *who*.

I believe that all truth is God's truth. So, as I read Brown's extensive research on the subject, I turned to Scripture to test it. Not only do I think that Brown is right, but suddenly, the Genesis story has become clearer to me than ever.

While Adam and Eve are flailing around in Genesis 3:9–13 with words of shame, hiding, fear, and blame, God goes straight to the heart of the real issue—their guilt. He begins his conversation with them by addressing their will-ful disobedience to his command. *"Have you eaten from the tree that I commanded you not to eat from?"*

And their response? In their effort to deflect guilt, they blame one another and the serpent.

This is a critical point. God *wants* them to understand and take responsibility for their *actions*. But because shame has taken hold, their broken response is to hide from the God who made them, ashamed of *who they are.*

What a tragedy! Our shame makes us hide from God and each other, rather than running to God to deal with our guilt. You see, feeling guilt after we have disobeyed God is not a broken response but a healthy one. *Sin* is bad, but *guilt* serves as an internal alarm, a signal to us that we need to not only turn away from our sinful disobedience but also assume accountability for it. We give in to our weakness for pornography, or illegal drugs, or inappropriate sexual activity. We cheat on our taxes or in a business transaction. We give in to anger, selfishness, or pettiness. We lie, gossip, or slander. And yes, we feel guilt. But it's clueing us to take responsibility for those wrong actions and run toward God, not away from him. Jesus paid for our guilt on the cross. He provided a way out—he provided repentance and salvation. We need to say, "What I did was wrong. I'm sorry, Lord—please forgive me." Saying that may be painful, but it's an important first step to getting your life back in order and restoring your relationship with God. He has provided the way to repair the damage those sins have done in our hearts and lives.

So because God knows how important that step is, he questions Adam and Eve about what they did—giving them the cue to accept responsibility for their disobedience. He is coaching them to admit their guilt. God knows that without confession, there can be no repentance and therefore no healing. But Adam and Eve blow their cue. Their response, instead, is to deflect their guilt and hide in their shame.

And don't we do the same? In our shame, we fear. We

hide. We make excuses for ourselves and blame others—all of the things Adam and Eve did. And in our brokenness, all of those things are easier for us than admitting our guilt, even to ourselves.

What a crafty enemy we have. Can you see it? The enemy knows that if he can cause us to hide ourselves—who God made us to be—that it also causes us to lose sight of our identity in God as his image-bearers. Then, because our view of ourselves has been diminished, we shrink from stepping into the destiny God created for us. That's a very effective strategy. Satan started using shame that day with Adam and Eve, and he continues to use it to this day.

Merriam-Webster's Dictionary defines *guilt* as "responsibility for a crime or for doing something bad or wrong." But it defines *shame* as "a painful emotion caused by consciousness of guilt, shortcoming, or impropriety" and "a condition of humiliating disgrace or disrepute."

A painful emotion, *a condition*. We know how true that is, don't we? Adam and Eve committed an act of wrongdoing (I did a bad thing), and their *consciousness of guilt* quickly led to the painful emotion of shame (I am bad).

What does Scripture say about our *do*? In a nutshell, it says, *"For all have sinned and fall short of the glory of God"* (Romans 3:23). Every one of us is guilty. No exceptions.

What does Scripture say about our *who*? It says, *"I am fearfully and wonderfully made"* (Psalm 139:14).

Did you catch that? It does *not* say, you are fundamentally flawed and worthless—the message of shame. It says you are fearfully and wonderfully made. It says you are an image-bearer of God (Genesis 1:27). Yes, our behavior and the behavior of others will fall short of God's standard. But that wrong behavior does not change our value or our worth.

I thank God that he already has a remedy for our broken *do* and our broken *who*! I'm taking you along on a journey to discover that. But first—and this is so critical for those of us who struggle with shame—we need to understand that it is not just our *own* sin that triggers guilt and shame.

Soiled by Sin

Sin is such a spoiler, such a violation of God's perfect design, that even when we are *subjected* to sin—whether as a victim of it or simply as a witness of it—we can still suffer shame as a result.

A father says to a daughter: "You're just like your no-good mother! I should have known you'd never be worth anything!"

A boy lets a girl know she "isn't hot enough."

The popular group of girls at school decide that another girl is fair game for their mean-spirited insults. And other students, who want to be popular themselves, follow suit, making that girl's daily life at school a nightmare.

People repeatedly make fun of our height or our weight or the sound of our voice.

A controlling boss never misses an opportunity to express scorn.

A thoughtless teacher points out how we never measure up.

A jealous "friend," in the throes of her own insecurity, makes a habit of telling us how bad we are at something—until finally we come to believe it, and simply don't do that thing anymore, even though we used to love it.

In all of these examples, we feel shame because of the way we are treated by others. Shame can give our lives a shape that is nothing like the shape of the life God desires for us. It is this shame we must learn to overcome if our lives are to become free to be all that God created us to be and to do all he's called us to do.

When We Confuse Guilt and Shame

Remember Emma playing hide and seek when she was two? Within a few short years, her story painted a tragic picture of that second type of shame—the kind you're subjected to when you witness it.

Her parents lived a lifestyle immersed in drug addiction, poverty, deception, and violence. By the time she was six, her home life had become so dangerous that she had to be removed and placed in the care of her grandma. Carol arranged for counseling sessions for Emma to begin her long road toward healing.

The counselor, sensitive to the girl's reticence to reveal all that she had witnessed and suffered, spent the first few months establishing trust, allowing Emma to set the pace of self-disclosure. Finally, some months later, during the drive to her counseling appointment, Emma, now seven, said to Carol, "I think today I'll tell about all the hitting."

When the counselor summoned her back to the office, Emma was so eager to reveal her long-kept secrets that she hurriedly grabbed Carol's hand and nearly pulled her down the hallway. But rather than sitting on the floor as usual to play with a few favorite toys that the counselor always had waiting for her, Emma sat trembling on the couch, crowding tightly against Carol's side. Now that the moment had arrived, her eagerness was melting into discomfort. Her eyes grew anxious and turned to the floor. She began to squirm and to wring her hands nervously. Then, to Carol's surprise, Emma slowly stood and did something she'd never done before. She crossed the room, went behind the counselor's upholstered chair, and crouched behind it.

Carol's heart lurched. Emma was hiding. But there were no giggles of joyful anticipation.

Emma spent the entire hour behind that chair. Rather than her typical expressive dialogue, she whispered cryptic partial phrases about fighting and screaming and destruction. As the counselor gently probed, filling in the blanks and asking questions, Emma, from her hiding place, would confirm or correct the counselor's wise guesses as to what she had experienced. Sometimes, when the words were too painful to say, Emma stepped out of hiding just long enough to act out a scene of two people punching and kicking one another, throwing and breaking things, pulling hair. She even mimed screams without making a sound; then she went back behind the chair to whisper what happened next.

Emma was hiding in shame.

Had she abused anyone? No, she had witnessed abuse.

Had she attacked her mother or father? No, they had attacked one another.

Had she broken furniture, kicked down doors, smashed prized possessions, torn out clumps of hair? No. Her parents had done all those things.

But Emma carried the shame of those actions. This precious seven-year-old, to use Brené Brown's definition, felt "the intensely painful experience of believing she was flawed and therefore unworthy of acceptance and belonging." And so, she hid.

Emma felt shame *for what had been done to her and what she had witnessed*. She didn't know the difference between guilt and shame. She didn't know who was responsible for what. All she knew for sure was that a terrible wrongness had happened that made her want to hide. She felt it so intensely that even though she *wanted* to tell the counselor, *wanted* to speak the secrets, she couldn't bear to be seen while she did, and she couldn't bear to say the words aloud. Even though she desperately wanted the truth to be told, all she could bear was to cryptically hint at it from a hiding place.

I know exactly how she felt. I too felt deep shame for what was done *to me* during the years I was sexually abused, mocked for my heritage, and chastised for my love of learning and leading.

Why is it that the one *sinned against* feels such shame? Because sin, when unleashed, is so insidious, is such a violation of how we were created to live, that it often leaves the perpetrator and the victim, and even the witness, feeling stained. We were not created for such ugly acts—not to do them, not to have them done to us, not to witness them. We were created to forever enjoy the good gifts of a loving Father in a paradise of his making. When exposed to a violation of God's intentions, we feel fouled, violated, soiled to the core of our being. Then shame wraps its deceitful tendrils around our hearts and whispers such lies as *I am unlovely, unlovable, worthless, repelling, ugly, repulsive, horrid, loathsome, offensive* . . . the list goes on and on. Those are lies. But when you are exposed to sin, either your own or a sinful act inflicted upon you by another, or the sin that has invaded our world and permeated our culture, its filth feels contagious. This is the power of shame.

Exposing Our Shame to the Light

But here is the power of truth.

We are of such great value and worth to the God who breathed us into being that God, knowing full well that Adam and Eve had disobeyed him, came calling for them— seeking them—in the garden.

Shame's power can be broken. In fact, its power *has been broken.* There is a key that will unfasten the shackles of shame that have bound and imprisoned you.

This key can unlock the shame of the wrongs you have done.

This key can unlock the shame of the wrongs done to you.

This key is the love of Jesus Christ, crucified and risen.

God sees. He knows. He forgives. He redeems. And he restores—regardless of what you have done, or of what has been done to you. He is calling to you to come out of hiding and into his grace—his unconditional acceptance. He has loved you . . . always. So much so that he sent his only Son, Jesus, to pay the price for your salvation—which includes your freedom from shame (John 3:16). Believing that love— believing he loves you—is opening up your heart to your healing and freedom that he purchased through his death, burial, and resurrection.

His love can't fail (1 Corinthians 13:8); you will always be able to depend on it. He loves you with an everlasting love that can't be taken away (Jeremiah 31:3).

And there's an astounding promise that comes with his love: There's nothing that can separate you from it—not even shame (Romans 8:35–39).

So will you hide or will you seek? I invite you to join me and seek. Even if, like Emma, you take those first steps out of hiding in whispers and half-spoken sentences, the moment you start to move toward God's unconditional love, your healing from shame will begin just as it did for her in that counseling session. God has not left us alone in the garden, hiding in shame. Rather, he steps into our lives and calls us by name, eager to embrace us just as we are. He calls us to a breathtaking journey from hiding to full restoration and fellowship with him.

Chapter 3

REACHING FOR FREEDOM

I know of one woman who made the daring choice to come out of hiding to seek the One she hoped could free her from her shame. But it meant taking the greatest risk of her life. I don't know her name, but I do know her story, and for those of us who know the power of shame to keep us in hiding—isolated and excluded from the life we long to live—she can be a guide. She shows us that when we are willing to take that risk and reach for Jesus, we receive something far greater than we'd dared to hope.

> *A large crowd . . . pressed around [Jesus]. And a woman was there who had been subject to bleeding for twelve years. She had suffered a great deal under the care of many doctors and had spent all she had; yet instead of getting better she grew worse. When she heard about Jesus, she came up behind him in the crowd and touched his cloak, because she thought, "If I just touch his clothes, I will be healed."*
>
> Mark 5:24–28

And so begins the story of the woman who, troubled by a ceaseless menstrual cycle—not a monthly flow but a *perpetual* flow—risked everything, even the worsening of the shame she already suffered, in one last-ditch effort to be healed.

As women, we can empathize with her physical misery, but to understand the severe shame and social impact of her condition, we must understand the very specific Jewish laws concerning her condition found in Leviticus 15:19–30. God had designed these laws to protect the people, to encourage physical health and hygiene, but sadly they became something the culture used to judge.

According to the law, during a woman's regular monthly flow, she was considered "unclean" for seven days, beginning the first day of her flow. Anywhere she sat or laid was also considered unclean—and if anyone else were even to touch where she sat or laid, they too would be unclean, required to perform a ritual bathing, and remain unclean until the evening of that day.

Every month, a woman having her period was a risk to everyone around her. And, according to the law, she remained in this unclean state for an additional day after her period ended! She was clean only after presenting two turtledoves or two pigeons to the priest for a ritual sacrifice.

But this woman, the woman in our story who was about to risk it all to reach Jesus, never experienced that final day. For years she had been unclean as defined by the law, hidden because of her persistent condition, and shamed by culture's response to her plight.

In order for us, as twenty-first-century women, to grasp

the impact of this law in her life, we need to understand a bit about the living conditions of women in first-century Palestine. They lived in homes with small rooms filled with extended family. There was no "personal space" and little privacy. Several generations of women would work together, starting before dawn, preparing food for the entire family. (My Greek mother would have loved that part—kitchen time for the girls!) As they worked, they talked—this was their time of bonding, of sharing their lives and feelings and hopes—but not the woman with the perpetual flow. While all the other women were gathered, working together, she was confined to solitude.

And this had been going on for twelve years. No wonder she had exhausted her resources on doctors! This woman's plight was desperate. She did not have a monthly cycle. She had a daily cycle. Can you imagine how weak she was from the loss of blood? The smell that surrounded her? The constant washing and changing and isolation? There were no tampons, no shower down the hall, no indoor plumbing to flush away the blood, no washing machine and dryer for the soiled linens. This condition defined every second of every day of her life.

And then, a glimmer of hope: She learned that Jesus was in her town. She had heard the stories of his great power and miracles. This Jesus was doing what doctors could not. The blind were seeing; the lame were walking. Maybe he could heal her!

Yet her hope must have been mingled with frustration and helplessness. How desperate she must have felt, sitting in the lonely room devoted to her constant uncleanness, knowing that the laws of her religion, zealously enforced, precluded her from going out into public. Imagine her thoughts . . . her feelings . . .

If only I could touch him. He has healed others—surely he could heal me as well. And yet I can't approach him without risking even greater shame and condemnation than I'm experiencing now. If only . . .

Her Hope . . . Her Faith

But hope, driven by the desire to be free from shame, is a powerful motivator! Slowly at first, probably awed and terrified by her own audacity, she began to formulate a plan—a plan that would take her into the crowds on the streets of her village along the shores of Galilee for the first time in more than a decade.

We can only guess at the details: How she must have covered herself to avoid being recognized and slipped away from her family home. How she made her way through the press of the crowd to be near him, brushing past others who now, according to the laws of the Torah, had been rendered unclean but were unaware of it. She must have felt so liberated to be finally out in public for the first time in years, yet terrified of being caught and exposed for fouling them all.

Did she know what she would say, how she would approach Jesus if she managed to get near him? Perhaps not—after all, it would have put her at great social risk to explain to him, in public, why she needed healing. We can only guess what was going through her mind.

But we don't have to guess at the steadfastness of her faith. *If I just touch his clothes, I will be healed,* she thought. She didn't say, "Maybe," or "If I'm lucky," or "What have I got to lose?" She said, "I will be healed." This woman had faith! And she was willing to risk absolutely everything to act on it.

Was it a spur-of-the-moment inspiration when, seeing him come near, she pushed through the crowd and touched just the barest hem of his clothes? What she touched—the fringe of his cloak—is significant. It was his *tzitzit*. The law of Moses instructed the Israelites to make fringes on the corners of their garments and to put a blue cord on the fringe at each corner (Numbers 15:38; Deuteronomy 22:12). This fringe—the *tzitzit*—was important and special. It was the most valuable garment a man owned, and was certainly his most personal. Only immediate family should ever touch a man's *tzitzit*. For someone other than a wife, parent, son, or daughter to touch the *tzitzit* of a man's cloak would be horrifying.

Yet she risked it, and knew at once that her certainty had been correct. Her bleeding stopped immediately; she could feel within her body that she had been healed of her condition. Can you imagine the thrill that shot through her?

But to her shock and terror, Jesus suddenly stopped, turned around, and said, "Who touched my clothes?"

Now she had done it.

First-century Palestine was a culture defined by honor

and shame. When Jesus said, "Who touched my clothes?" this desperate woman knew that if she were discovered, she would disgrace not only herself, her family, and all her relatives, but also her neighbors. For twelve years, she had experienced the isolation and shame of uncleanness. Now she would be cursed with the humiliation of a public disgrace that she had brought upon her entire community.

Her act of courage is astounding. *"Then the woman, knowing what had happened to her, came and fell at his feet and, trembling with fear, told him the whole truth"* (Mark 5:33).

What integrity! What a risk! What boldness fueled by hope and faith. She exposed herself as the culprit. She knew that she would be disgraced, and once those in the crowd realized that they had been exposed to her uncleanness, despised. She could have hidden in the crowd. Yet, *knowing what had happened to her,* awed and grateful that she'd been healed, she stepped forward and confessed. She moved toward Jesus rather than away from him. It was worth it to her, so grateful and relieved was she to finally be rid of the perpetual shame of being unclean.

And then something amazing happened. Something she surely couldn't have anticipated in her wildest dreams. Of all the words Jesus could have spoken to her, he chose as his first word:

"Daughter."

Remember, only a member of a man's immediate family was allowed the intimate act of touching his *tzitzit.* With this one word, Jesus removed from her any blame for her act of faith.

"Daughter," he said to her, *"your faith has healed you. Go in peace and be freed from your suffering"* (Mark 5:34).

Daughter! How stunning! She had come to find relief from her suffering—and not only was she healed, *she was given a new identity!* Jesus embraced her into his family, making her not only acceptable but intimately and tenderly connected to him.

Daughter.

He took away not only her illness and isolation but also her shame. Jesus not only restored her to health and to community, but he called her family.

He was not ashamed of her! He bestowed upon her dignity and value. He esteemed her in a society where a woman, judged far less than equal to a man, was considered private property. He lifted not only the shame of her physical condition but far, far more—he lifted the shame of her lack of societal value, her lack of worth.[1]

Such a short story, with so much meaning that speaks to every one of us who carries shame—and that is every one of us. After all, there is more than one way to bleed.

I Too Grew Tired of Bleeding

"Go in peace and be freed from your suffering." Is that what you long for? I did! Oh, how I longed for peace. My shame-filled life was anything but peaceful. It was filled with striving to prove myself, to protect myself, and to quiet constant whispers of shame.

I'd been curious about God since I was a child. I had grown up in a very formal church, and as a teen was intrigued and even warmed by what little I knew of God. One day, after some Christian speakers visited my public school, I made a decision for Christ. I wanted to have what they had, to follow him as they did. But in truth, as time went by, I was aware of a huge disparity between what I wanted and how I was living. I certainly knew I wasn't following him. Although I wanted to do what was right, I was a textbook case of what happens to an unhealed, wounded, shamed soul. The high school girl I was, so wounded and broken, lost in hiding myself on so many levels, chose many aimless directions.

I sought the affirmation I craved and the intimacy I longed for in all the wrong places. I kept cycling in and out of patterns of destructive behavior and poor relational decisions because I was looking for freedom—even though I didn't know I was bound.

By the time I hit my university years, I was so shackled by shame that I had completely lost my way. I had descended from being the victim of shameful acts perpetrated by others to being adrift in a shameless lifestyle of my own choosing. My wounded heart had become hardened. To protect my heart from ever being hurt again, I emotionally isolated myself.

Like Adam and Eve hiding from God in the garden, I pushed God onto the back burner of my life, instead choosing destructive relationships I hoped would fill the void. I hid from him and myself. But God didn't give up on me. He kept turning my thoughts back to him time and time again.

Distraught, feeling that my life was out of control, I decided to take a two-year break from university to travel the world with friends. I knew that I was going in search of something—but of what, I wasn't sure. At nineteen, I had no sense of purpose. I only knew that life wasn't working for me, and that I constantly yearned for more.

On my twenty-first birthday, a couple of girlfriends and I were staying at a friend's home in Zurich, Switzerland. They were partying, but I was in no such mood. I'd always anticipated that turning twenty-one would be exciting, filled with promise, so the reality of turning twenty-one in a state of despair hit me hard. If my trip had been an attempt to run away from my problems, I could now see that I'd brought my broken, hopeless, self-serving, meaningless life with me. Despondent, I left the party and stepped out onto the balcony to be alone with my thoughts.

There I sat in the brilliant midday sunshine on a balcony in Zurich. I wanted to be filled with excitement and a sense of adventure, but I felt miserable and desperate. This trip was not turning out to be the life-changing adventure I'd hoped it would be. My life, empty of meaning, was a tangled mess of guilt and shame, blame and fear. Now, on my milestone birthday, loathing the emptiness my poor choices had yielded, I ached for a life that mattered. I knew little about the Bible and even less about the purpose of my life. All I knew for sure was that the life I was living was taking me further away from God, not closer to him—and I wanted to be closer.

"God, I don't even know what life truly is—but I do

know that what I've been living isn't life. I've done so many bad things, I'm guessing that you could never forgive me. I suppose I'm going to hell—but can I spend what's left of my life making sure other people don't have to? Maybe I can really help them. At least my life will matter somehow."

My expectation that I was going to hell sounds hopeless and unbiblical. But because I'd grown up in a religious culture that seemed to teach only judgment—"If you do that, God won't love you and you'll go to hell"—I had no understanding of grace. Based on my track record, I assumed that someone like me had no hope of heaven—another one of shame's lies—but there must be plenty of others who still had a chance. Did I mention that I was messed up? I'm so glad that my mess did not deter Jesus.

The more I thought about helping others, the faster my heart pounded. Because self-absorbed living was taking me nowhere, I figured I would offer selfless living to God. I drew from the only models I knew of what I supposed to be a godly life—nuns and missionaries. God-workers in my understanding. I reasoned that to please God, I needed to do some sort of good works.

Though externally my life was still a mess, in my heart I felt an inexplicable shift. I was suddenly convinced that good works, becoming a God-worker, was the answer. I felt an urge to get started.

Of course, I didn't yet understand what it meant to submit myself to the lordship of Jesus Christ. I had no idea what contribution discipleship, regular Bible study, or a transforming Christian community could make to my life. I couldn't even have shaped the questions to find those things out, because I lacked the concepts. I simply was convinced that I needed to work hard to prove to God that I was serious about my decision to follow him. Having only known a religious system based on being good in order to earn God's love and acceptance made this idea seem perfectly logical and rational to me. I had never known unconditional love. I had never felt good enough—and was always trying to work harder and to act better so that I would be accepted, loved, and valued. I had grown up hearing phrases like:

"Christine, if you do that, God will punish you."

"Christine, God will not love you if you say those things."

So I carried those concepts and behaviors into my new relationship with Jesus. I felt that I could make up for all the things I had done wrong by doing good works for the rest of my life.

But here's the irony: Even though my theology was broken and my reasoning wrong, I had arrived at one core truth of the Christian life: We *are* called to join God in his work on this earth.

My decision instantly lit a flame of passion in my soul. I was on the same balcony in Switzerland, but with an entirely different heart. My despondency had fled, and I sensed a stirring connection with God, a spine-tingling sense of his power and presence.

How do you explain a God-encounter like that? I know of only one explanation—the touch of God on my heart. I had risked confessing I was soiled and unclean, and rather than judgment, I found open arms.

Daughter.

Words of resolve came tumbling out of me. "God, I'll do whatever you want," I said aloud. "I'll work in some soup kitchen for the rest of my life, handing out food to homeless people." My mind flashed on Mother Teresa. "Maybe I'll go find lepers and work with them. Or the desperately poor. Whatever it costs, I'll do it. I want my life to matter."

I assumed that this choice meant massive changes to life as I knew it. And yet without reservation, I was 100 percent willing. "Whatever I have to give up, whatever relationships have to end, I'm all in, God."

I decided on the spot to go back home to Australia—immediately—to get started. No matter what relational mess awaited me there. No matter how ashamed I was of my past. I still had to complete my final year of school, but that wouldn't stop me either; I would get started on being a God-worker right away. I assumed that this would mean walking away from the possibilities of wealth, career, marriage, family—any of the trappings of normal life. And that was fine by me. I'd never known wealth anyway, and relationships had brought me nothing but trouble. I was ready.

I ran into the house and announced my decision to my friends.

"Do what? Are you crazy? Now? Don't leave! Think this over. Slow down."

Before that transforming encounter with God on the balcony, I would have felt embarrassed as my friends scoffed at my decision. But now, their vehement protests didn't faze me. Instead, even as they urged me to stay, I felt a weight lifting from my heart and my passion growing stronger. I was sure that, to answer this call and leave behind the behaviors that had taken me down my destructive path, I would have to ignore not just these voices but many others urging me to reconsider. Was I desperate enough to risk the loss of friends and the sense of belonging? Definitely! I wanted to be free of shame! I started packing.

I was tired of bleeding. Hope had been ignited. My desperation had turned to faith. Now, I was reaching for freedom.

What We Don't Reveal Can't Heal

The story of the woman with the issue of blood speaks to each of us. The power that healed her is available to us as well. That's why I love this story! We all have shame wounds that are bleeding, and nothing we've done—no passage of time, no procedure, no ritual, no conversation or compensation— has been successful in closing them. Whether the cause of our shame was forced upon us or was the result of a choice we freely made—or as in my case, both—each of us bears that wound, that secret, that blemish. We feel unclean. But as the woman who took her shame to Jesus—who risked stepping out of the house, who in fear and trembling reached deep into her well of courage and confessed her need for him right there in public—found healing, we can too.

I did . . . even though I felt powerful reluctance as my journey progressed.

It's ironic, but the strongest resistance to the process of healing from shame is shame itself. We're ashamed to admit that we need healing, that we have been damaged in ways that cause us shame. But to be healed, we must acknowledge *all* of our wounds. The journey from shame to freedom and a full life in Christ must be a blatantly honest, nothing-hidden voyage.

Like me, you probably spent years covering up your shame wounds—so why would you now want to uncover them and look at them? When you're suffering from shame, the *last* thing you want to do is make yourself vulnerable. Your vulnerability is one of the reasons you're suffering from shame in the first place—so why would you want to open yourself up for more?

Because what we don't reveal can't be healed. Our wounds need treatment, and the only way they'll be healed is if we acknowledge them, uncover them, and hold them up to the One who can help.

But here's the challenge: We've been shackled in the dark for so long that the darkness has crippled and immobilized us. We need the light of God to shine on us—shackles, shame, and all. The entrance of his Word gives light (Psalm 119:130). That light is the understanding that sets us free. Until we let in the light—the truth—we will remain hindered, unable to fulfill our potential.

The apostle Paul teaches in Ephesians 5 that bringing what's hidden in the dark—our secrets of shame—into the light, into God's merciful presence, is how they lose their power over us.

For you were once darkness, but now you are light in the Lord. Live as children of light (for the fruit of the light consists in all goodness, righteousness and truth) and find out what pleases the Lord. Have nothing to do with the fruitless deeds of darkness, but rather expose them. It is shameful even to mention what the disobedient do in secret. But everything exposed by the light becomes visible—and everything that is illuminated becomes a light.

Ephesians 5:8–13

God's light is tender, not harsh. As you trust him with your pain, he will gently shine his healing light on all your wounds. He is for you, not against you—and will never shame you or humiliate you (Romans 8:31). That kind of treatment is not in his nature. He is good, merciful, and kind. He didn't cause your pain, but he's ready to help you through it.

Jesus paid for your guilt and bore your shame. He carried it all to the cross. *But there he left it!*

He has borne our griefs, sicknesses, weaknesses, and distresses . . .
  He carried our sorrows and pains . . .
  He was wounded for our transgressions . . .
  He was bruised for our guilt and iniquities . . .
  The chastisement needful to obtain peace and well-being for us was upon Him . . .

> *With the stripes that wounded Him we are healed*
> *and made whole.*
>
> Isaiah 53:4–5 AMP

His death, burial, and resurrection were more than enough for you—for all of us. When he emerged from that tomb, he was no longer clothed in the sin and shame of this world. Sin and its shame were left entombed. Conquered. Vanquished. Paid for. Redeemed by his blood sacrifice. It is finished. The blood of Jesus has healed you. The blood of Jesus has set you free. Jesus was wounded for *your* healing; he bore *your* shame so *you* could live free (1 Peter 2:24).

So, will you remain in hiding or will you, like the bleeding woman, like me, seek Jesus to heal your guilt and shame? Will you risk living free?

God answered my cry and called me daughter.

He calls you daughter as well.

That is why he came.

Chapter 4

WOMAN ON PURPOSE

My balcony encounter with Jesus was just that—an encounter. I had no idea where it would lead, but in my heart I knew it was somewhere better than where I'd been. I love how Jesus leads us—even when we know nothing. He led me in my heart to go home and begin my road to freedom.

To the best of my limited understanding, I immediately began living for God instead of for myself. I served at-risk young people at a Christian youth center and went back to school to complete my degree. As a "God-worker," I defaulted to "works" because that was all I knew—consciously and subconsciously. My heart was right, but my shame-based nature was always working for approval—including God's.

After my first few months at the youth center, John, a friend and fellow volunteer, invited me to church. That very week I had been reading the book of Hebrews and came across this verse: *"And let us consider how we may spur one another on toward love and good deeds, not giving up meeting together, as some are in the habit of doing, but encouraging one another—and all the more as you see the Day approaching"* (Hebrews 10:24–25).

I saw this as a sign from God, and because I was so desperate to please him, I said yes. This is how I ended up walking into Hills Christian Life Center, what the world now knows as Hillsong Church in Sydney.

From the moment I walked in the door, I felt that I had found the home I didn't even know I was looking for. Everything was unlike anything I had ever experienced in church, but somehow it felt so familiar, safe, and right. There, immersed in fellowship and worship, mentored in God's Word, loved, valued, and accepted, I became so alive and on fire with purpose.

I received God's Word like a thirsty sponge, soaking it in as fast as I could, realizing for the first time how parched my soul had been. I initially had thought serving God was all about what I was doing for God and this broken, hurting world. But all the while, God knew that my inner world was just as broken and hurting—and needed to be restored. Slowly, it dawned on me that while I was busy serving God, God was busy transforming me—from the inside out. He wasn't just working *through* me—he was also working *in* me. Because of sound teaching and loving leadership, for the first time in my life, I was beginning to understand what guilt— healthy guilt—really was, and grasping that the blood of Jesus was the only remedy for it.

Shame, however, was a far greater mystery for me to unravel. Having lived immersed in shame my entire life, I had a very broken *who*.

Yes, a very broken *who*.

I was often surprised in the midst of my newfound joy to find myself plagued by shame—even though I didn't call it that back then. I just knew it as feelings of insecurity and fear, of not being or doing not enough. Like many new believers, I had assumed that once I committed my life to Jesus all my old struggles—and the feelings that went with them—would evaporate. And sometimes, I think we try to outrun them by doing as many good works as possible. But that doesn't make them go away either. I soon discovered there was a reason that when Jesus called the twelve apostles, he spent the next three years discipling them. Spiritual depth—maturity and freedom—requires spiritual growth, and growth takes time. There's a process to go through. Salvation is just the door to what is possible. It is the key to finding deliverance and freedom.

Feeling Less Than

Over time, I dealt with issues as God showed them to me, but I experienced so much shame in my inner world that I didn't recognize a shame that I had struggled with my entire life. I often felt that as a woman, I was secondary. I was *less than*. For years, I would have vehemently denied it, but I was deceived, because it showed up in so many areas. It affected my thinking about my leadership and ministry. It affected how I interacted with others. It clouded my ability to be my authentic self. I was tempted to pull back, step aside, or diminish my roles because of shame-filled feelings I'd had as long as I could remember.

Once, during a difficult conversation, my mom said she had always loved me—and my brothers—before we were ever born. It was a moment I'll never forget. I believed her, but deep down I never felt that I measured up to my parents' expectations. They were excited when I was born and thrilled to have a daughter—their little girl—but I was simply wired differently from anything they expected. So I always felt like a failure as a daughter.

In the interest of full disclosure, I'm quite sure I was not an easy kid to parent. In fact, I am absolutely sure I wasn't. My parents deserve a gold medal for trying. They were great and loving parents, but we were a part of a culture that dictated girls would act a certain way and boys another. The only problem was, as I have already told you, ballet and knitting were really not my passions. This led to numerous "heated discussions" with my mom during my teenage years, and lots of time alone in my room to "think about my choices." The problem was I was into sports and books, justice and global issues, learning and leading—all things assigned to boys in my culture, not girls.

I'd been taught that a Greek woman's role was to stay within the boundaries of keeping a clean house, raising kids, and making life comfortable for a husband. (These are good and meaningful roles! But there was so much more inside of me than these roles.) I was not encouraged to pursue higher education or my dreams, because once I married, I would have no use for either. I had fought against the underlying message all my life that as a woman—as a good Greek girl—I should limit my horizons and temper my ambitions.

I know that some of you cannot fathom that this was my reality in light of what I am doing today, but I can assure you that it was. I also know I am not alone. I talk to women in nations all over the world on a weekly basis, and many have bought into the lie that we are the second sex, that we do not matter *as much* as men, that we have clearly defined roles as women, and that we are not gifted *as importantly* as men.

Women from all walks of life have confided in me their own struggles with this kind of shame—from CEOs of large corporations to sales clerks at the mall, from leaders of effective ministries to volunteers in the church kitchen, from single gals nurturing careers to stay-at-home moms to working moms juggling long to-do lists. A shocking number of women struggle with the sense that somehow, as women, they are *less than*.

But woman, God created you on purpose, for a purpose. He did not make a mistake when he made us women. He made us intentionally, not accidentally. We were predestined, predetermined, and preordained to be who we are—divine creations (Genesis 1). God carefully and by design placed gifts and talents within us, and he has called us to activate and use them to bring him great glory during our time on this earth as we influence and lead others to him (John 15:8). We are a gift—an expression of who he is—and the world needs what he has deposited in us. He does not want us to be restricted by cultural limitations—or any kind of limitations—but rather to unleash us and all of our potential into our kingdom purpose.

God has always honored and esteemed women—his feminine creation. We need only look to Jesus' behavior to see how God has valued us. Jesus dignified every woman, compassionately bringing them out of hiding and lifting shame off them. He demonstrated unconditional love for every woman he ministered to, never treating anyone as less than. He even overshadowed them with love and protected those who made mistakes. Women like the one caught in adultery.

Shame Meets the Mercy of Jesus

At dawn one morning, Jesus went to the temple to teach. The people gathered round, ready to be taught—but the Pharisees rushed up, bringing a woman with them. *"Teacher, this woman was caught in the act of adultery,"* they said (John 8:4).

My heart catches at the thought of what this woman must have been feeling. Can you imagine her fear? And above all, her humiliation? Caught in the act, yanked from under the covers, dragged through the streets under the stares of her neighbors. Was she covering her face, crying, pleading, silent? We don't know. But she had to be aware that there would be no erasing the damage now done to her reputation, that she would from this day forward be the subject of whispers and fodder for the town gossips. She had, after all, been caught in the act. She had violated the law.

We know nothing of what may have driven her to this. Was she a repeat offender? Had she been seduced, perhaps even pressured or forced, by an unscrupulous man? Did she give in, in a moment of weakness, to something that she thought might bring her some relief in a loveless marriage? The Bible doesn't say. What led her to commit adultery is not the point of the story, but rather Jesus' response to her when her shameful adultery was publicly exposed.

We cannot help but notice that only the woman was brought before Jesus. Isn't someone conspicuously missing from the scene? Apparently, only the woman—not her lover—was considered enough of an offender to be brought to the temple for immediate judgment. For a woman, adultery was not just a cause of deep shame but also potentially a capital offense.

The Pharisees challenged Jesus: *"In the Law Moses commanded us to stone such women. Now what do you say?"* (John 8:5).

The Bible doesn't leave any doubt about what these men were attempting to do. This wasn't a matter of wanting to adhere to the purest interpretation of justice according to the law. They were using this question as a trap, in order to have a basis for accusing him (John 8:6). This woman was their bait. Would Jesus give a nod to stoning her, or disregard the law? *Either way,* they must have thought, *we win.*

Jesus didn't take the bait. And notice how cleverly he distracted the attention of the crowd from the humiliated woman; he knelt and wrote on the ground with his finger.

Imagine the crowd's puzzlement as they watched him. The Pharisees probably looked at each other, confused, and remained silent for a few moments to see whether he would speak. When he didn't, they began assaulting him with questions again, and eventually he stood and uttered the lines that have echoed through the minds of people of conscience ever since: *"Let any one of you who is without sin be the first to throw a stone at her"* (John 8:7). And he knelt and wrote on the ground again.

What was it that he was writing on the ground? A list of the sins of those who stood in judgment? The name of the missing man? It would be fascinating to find out, but that's not what impresses me most about these verses. I find it a measure of Jesus' mercy toward the woman that, once again, he draws all eyes away from her and toward himself as he knelt.

I try to imagine myself in the woman's place, dragged from the warmth of a bed with perhaps just time enough to snatch a garment or a blanket before being hauled through the streets to stand before Jesus and a hostile, glaring, condemning crowd, already hefting their stones. But for a few precious moments, she senses that no one is looking at her. All eyes are on Jesus. He has interceded for her already—and he hasn't said anything to her yet. As he would one day soon on the cross, he has taken all her shame and humiliation on himself and given her a respite.

As if this weren't relief enough, what happened next must have astonished her even more. The crowd of people began to drift away—*"the older ones first,"* the Bible tells us (John 8:9).

Jesus didn't stand until the crowd had dispersed. Then

he turned to the woman and said, *"Woman, where are they? Has no one condemned you?"* (John 8:10).

Don't you imagine it was with equal parts relief and amazement that she said, *"No one, sir."*

Have you ever wondered how God reacts when you fall into sin? Then listen to these gentle words of Jesus and let them echo in your heart: *"Then neither do I condemn you. Go now and leave your life of sin"* (John 8:11).

We don't know whether any other women were present in the temple courts to witness this exchange, but even if not, surely there were women who witnessed the woman being dragged through the streets by the Pharisees. How grateful and appreciative they must have felt toward this man who actually protected her and showed compassion, as no other men—including, apparently, the man who'd been sleeping with her—were doing.

Women Are Not "Less Than"

One could argue that the woman was brought for judgment because of her sin, but that would be only partly true. If justice had been the real goal, then the man would have been charged as well. No, this woman was guilty of the crime of being a *woman* caught in adultery.

If that sounds like an exaggeration, it wasn't one by much in first-century Israel. Women in that culture were second-class citizens at best, akin to slaves. Men had complete authority over their wives and daughters and made all decisions regarding relationships and activities. The Mishnah, part of the Jewish Talmud, taught that women were like Gentile slaves and could be obtained by intercourse, money, or written contract. Women had few rights inside the home and practically none outside of it. They were not counted as members during a synagogue count, and received little or no religious education, except from their husband if he so desired. Men were discouraged from speaking to women on the street.

First-century Palestine—the world into which Jesus was born—was clearly a male-dominated society, but it certainly hasn't been the only one. I can point out another one from personal experience: Greek culture. In the Greek family I was raised in, I felt that because I was neither the firstborn nor a son, I was somehow "less than." "You're only a woman," I was told in so many ways—and it was crystal clear that this was not a good thing.

Nowhere in my experience has the denigration of women been clearer as in our work through A21 to rescue sex-trafficked women. In one court case, the accused was asked by the judge, "Why do you traffic women?"

The man shrugged. "They are easier to traffic than drugs and guns," he said. "The penalty is not as harsh, and you can kick them like an animal, and they will do what you want them to do."

Misogyny. It's an ugly word—the hatred of women or girls. It comes to us through governments, cultures, religions, and nations. We'd like to think that it's something that happens elsewhere, far away, or a long time ago. But no other word describes so precisely the attitude of the trafficker on trial that day, nor of the industry he represents. And it shows up in many other ways as well, from jokes—have you ever heard a blonde joke about a dumb blond man?—to pornography, to the difficulty a woman has getting equal pay for equal work, to the ease with which crimes against women are ignored or covered up.

Women are denigrated as often in modern society as they were in ancient cultures. Two children are sold into the human sex trade every minute. Nearly two million children are forced into the worldwide sex trade every year.[1] And 80 percent of all trafficking victims are women and girls.[2] According to the United Nations, there are one hundred million women missing worldwide[3]—and five thousand girls are murdered around the world every year by their parents for acting in ways that shame their family.[4]

The history of our world—all periods of history, all continents, all cultural traditions—is rampant with damage, oppression, diminishment, contempt, and hostility aimed at women. Just think of the Salem witch trials, for example. Even today, women are stoned to death for adultery in India and Pakistan; they are raped and sold as slaves in Syria. And the men who perpetrate these horrendous acts are excused with religious theology. In every case, in every century, women have been targets. I see this same kind of evil played out in A21 court cases all the time.

Of all places on earth, the Christian church could be the most significant place of healing and hope—the place where women experience the joys of being respected, appreciated, esteemed, included, and celebrated. After all, God himself made women in his own image—"male and *female* he created them" (Genesis 1:26–27, emphasis added). What a profound thought: God's image is only fully reflected in both man and woman. When we denigrate a woman, we are in fact diminishing part of the image of God. When we exclude women, we exclude part of God. When we put women down, we tarnish the image of God.

Psalm 139:13 tells us, *"You knit me together in my mother's womb."* God took just as much time and care knitting together every female child as he did every male child. Male and female are equally loved and valued by him. Paul wrote to the Galatians stating this very point: *"There is neither Jew nor Gentile, neither slave nor free, nor is there male and female, for you are all one in Christ Jesus"* (Galatians 3:28, emphasis added).

In Christ, there is no distinction in value between male and female.

No one dignifies, affirms, and celebrates women like the God of the Bible. Therefore, it should be the church that leads the way and sets the example of placing value upon womanhood . . . of getting them to Jesus, who can lift their shame and set them free. My friend Dianne wanted all of this. Her story is painful, and her triumph is inspiring.

Dianne

Dianne grew up deeply affected by her stepfather's view of women, and it later affected her career and ministry.

"I knew that my stepdad loved me—he would make a point of telling me so. But he also made it very, very clear that he thought women were subservient to men. I could have said, 'Dad, you're being unreasonable. That isn't true. Look at this woman, who has become a leader in her field. Or that woman, who heads up a Fortune 500 company, or this one, who's a senator.' But I didn't. I just swallowed it. Why? Because I was inclined to believe him."

An honor student, Dianne remembers one particular family dinner during her high-school years when she began to excitedly discuss options for where she would attend college. Her stepdad looked at her mom and said, "I will not invest one dime in Dianne's college education. Girls go to college for one reason: to find husbands. Once they get married and have babies, they never use their degree anyway. That's a huge investment for something that she doesn't need and that will never be used."

But driven by her passion, Dianne put herself through college, then found a position working under a male boss who believed, as Dianne's dad had, that women were *less than* men. "I'll never forget," Dianne says, "the day he told me, 'Dianne, you have to understand—the Bible says that *men* are the glory of God. And women are the glory of men. So it wouldn't honor God if I paid you as much as I pay the men who work here.' And he didn't. Understand that the two men he was paying $10,000 a year more than he paid me didn't have college degrees and also didn't have experience in our field.

"He leased a brand-new car for each of them, because he felt that would glorify God. Meanwhile, somebody had donated a clunker to the organization. I suppose some would have argued that the one female on the team—who, incidentally, had twice the territory to cover as either of my two male colleagues—should have had a car that wouldn't break down and leave her stranded, that perhaps God wouldn't be pleased with placing the one woman on the team in danger. Not my boss. His comment: 'You get this car, Dianne, because God wouldn't be pleased with me if I made the men on my team drive around in this junky car.' And if I had a problem with that, he said, then it was because I didn't have a submissive, gentle spirit, and that was something I needed to work on."

Dianne bought that reasoning. "I thought it was my issue; that my heart was selfish and prideful and I needed a softer heart. Besides, I really did like my two male colleagues. They were like brothers to me. I didn't even resent that they were making more money, because after all, they were men and I was *just* a woman."

Do you hear the shame Dianne had internalized based on the fact she was a woman?

"It wounded me to hear that men were the glory of God, while I was only the glory of man. Because *I so wanted God to be proud of me!* And, yes, I wanted my boss to be proud of me too."

So many women, *too many women*, squirm with discomfort when trying to resolve the apparent conflict between being fully themselves—using the best of their gifts, skills and passions—and their concept of what it means to be a woman, to be called daughter.

Jesus' Unconditional Love toward Women

Jesus saw the woman caught in adultery as a beloved daughter, his creation, someone to be nurtured and enabled, someone for whom he was willing to die, someone for whom he had a vital purpose and destiny. He entered a male-dominated culture that devalued women, and to the consternation of the powerful men around him, he talked to women, addressed their concerns, healed them, forgave them their sins, and treated them with respect. Imagine the impact this had on women treated as slaves for so long!

Jesus *engaged* with women throughout his ministry. At a time when Jewish men—and especially rabbis—had nothing to do with women in public, even their own wives, Jesus esteemed women, touched women, spoke to women, taught women, and as we saw in John 8, interceded for and protected women.

He *welcomed women to minister to him.* Physically touching

him, washing his feet, anointing him with oil. Rather than rebuke them, as the Pharisees wanted, he affirmed them.

And to top it all off, *women ministered with him.* They traveled with him and helped fund his ministry. In a seldom mentioned passage from Luke 8, just before the parable of the sower, Luke says:

> *After this, Jesus traveled about from one town and village to another, proclaiming the good news of the kingdom of God. The Twelve were with him, and also some women who had been cured of evil spirits and diseases: Mary (called Magdalene) from whom seven demons had come out; Joanna the wife of Chuza, the manager of Herod's household; Susanna; and many others. These women were helping to support them out of their own means.*
>
> Luke 8:1–3

Don't miss the exciting implications of this quiet passage. Women—some of them married, and apparently some of them not—were not only traveling with Jesus and his disciples but also, grateful and joyful that they had been healed of their diseases or freed from demonic oppression, were supporting Jesus' ministry from their own funds. That means, first, that they *had* their own funds, and second, that they had the freedom to dispose of those funds as they saw fit. In the male-controlled society those women lived in, that is nothing short of remarkable. We know from biblical accounts that even some of Jesus' own disciples saw this as unseemly, even scandalous.

They were chosen to be the very first to bear the most powerful message in the history of mankind, the axis of our Christian faith, the event that makes Christianity Good News and not just good advice: "He is risen from the dead!"

In a time when a woman's testimony was not valid in a Jewish court, when women were not permitted to be legal witnesses; in a time when there was no social media to capture the moment, Jesus entrusted women to be the very first ones to go and tell the disciples that Jesus was risen from the dead. And the disciples then went and told the world.

There's a powerful understanding here: Jesus wanted *women* to go and tell. This was planned. This was intentional. He knew who would come looking. He did not expect women to be silent, hidden, withdrawn, or invisible. As he had done numerous times prior to his death, he valued, esteemed, and included women. He entrusted the Good News to be delivered by women. (Truthfully, I think he knew that if you wanted a message spread—back then or today—just tell a woman! In twenty-four hours, it will have gone viral!)

When I think about what Jesus did, and reflect on the serious assignment he gave those women, I feel like I'm one of them. Jesus lifted shame off me, and so today, I can't help but want to go and tell everyone that he is alive. I want women everywhere to experience the same freedom I enjoy.

I believe you feel the same way, because once shame is lifted off you, you can't keep this Good News to yourself. You want to be included in the Great Commission, filling every person's life in your sphere of influence with his message of salvation and freedom. You want every woman to know that whoever believes in him will *never* be put to shame (Romans 10:11). You aren't able to hold yourself back from telling every woman *all* of the Good News …

Fear is banished (1 John 4:18).

Love is stronger than death (Romans 6:9).

Good triumphs over evil (2 Corinthians 2:14).

Our needs can be met in Christ (Philippians 4:19).

Captives can be set free (Luke 4:18).

Hope can be restored (Romans 5:5).

Diseases can be healed (Matthew 8:17).

Peace can prevail (John 14:27).

Joy can reign (John 16:24).

Failures can be redeemed (Romans 8:28).

Jesus has entrusted you and me purposefully to share this news with a lost and dying world—so let's put off shame and put on Christ so that no one misses out on hearing it. Go and tell!

Chapter 5

YOU GET TO CHOOSE

I stood in the magnificent Great Hall of the University of Sydney, shoulder to shoulder with my fellow graduates, all dressed in black robes with square caps balanced precariously on our heads. As the majestic notes of the pipe organ filled the vast hall, my eyes swept upward to the heights of the weathered stained-glass windows, then back down over the polished wooden pews filled to overflowing with the family and friends of my graduating class. One hundred and fifty years of rich tradition, and now I was part of the story of this place. We'd made it. *I'd* made it.

As I took in all the splendor of the moment, many of my fellow graduates scanned the crowd of guests, trying to spot parents and siblings who'd come to celebrate their academic accomplishments. But I wasn't looking for my family. They weren't there. My dad had died a few years earlier, and I hadn't even told the others that today was my graduation day. It had now been a long time since my mom had said anything negative about my pursuit of education, but I didn't want to face even the chance of that kind of pain on this day. Despite the recent positive changes in my life, I was still broken enough that I didn't want to risk the rejection I would feel if no one showed up! So I didn't give them an opportunity.

Looking back, I suspect that my mother would have been there and been proud of me. She'd have been smiling and waving, with other family members by her side. But shame kept me from ever being able to know for sure.

I hadn't expected to care whether my family was there that day, but as the organ music subsided and the ceremony began, the growing lump in my throat exposed the hurt I was trying to choke back. An unexpected old wound I'd thought had healed was still bleeding. I *did* care. And although I hadn't given my family even a chance to attend, their absence felt like a flashing neon light over my head: *Unloved! Unworthy! Uncelebrated!* Or was that self-pity I was feeling? Or resentment or even anger? When would the hurt of old shame stop?

I was discovering that there were pockets of shame still hidden in the corners of my heart that I didn't want to deal with. They were painful. Embarrassing. Just too much to face . . .

But eventually, to be free, I had to face them. I had to acknowledge them, expose them to the light, and let the unconditional love of Jesus heal me . . . like it had the women in the Bible. It was a matter of courage and choice—and it still is today whenever he reveals any hidden shame to me. The more we are conformed and transformed into the image of Christ, the more we shed the debilitating effects of shame that cause aspects of our lives to remain in hiding.

My life was messy from my earliest memories, and my journey is still messy at times. But Jesus called me daughter while I was still messy—and he made me feel loved, wanted, and cherished—something I had never felt before. Calling me daughter lifted the shame of abandonment, adoption, and abuse—of not being the daughter anyone ever wanted. Once the shame was lifted, I had the power to choose to walk in my new identity as a daughter of the king instead of as a victim of my past. Jesus had set me free from shame, but I had to choose to stand up and walk out of my unlocked prison cell, drop off my unshackled chains, and step into the future shame-free.

This is always much easier said than done. Being set free and walking in freedom are not the same. The first was done for us by Jesus, but the second we must choose to do ourselves in his strength and by his grace.

The Power to Choose

The power of choice is one of the greatest gifts God has given us as his image-bearers. People controlled by shame often feel that they don't have that power—that their lives are limited by the circumstances of their past, or the control or scrutiny of others. Therefore, they often feel that their future is completely out of their hands. I felt this way for many years; that my history would define my destiny because

I'd been abused. Abuse, by its very nature, is perpetrated by someone stronger—either physically or psychologically—on someone weaker or less powerful. Because of this, abuse makes a person feel powerless. But when I discovered I could actually choose for myself, that was a huge revelation. The truth of God's Word brought me new light and strength:

> *I have set before you life and death, blessings and curses.*
> *Now choose life, so that you and your children may live*
> *and that you may love the LORD your God, listen to his*
> *voice, and hold fast to him.*
>
> Deuteronomy 30:19–20

It was as if a lightbulb turned on! I saw that I did not need to remain a victim. No, I could not change the past—neither what happened to me nor what I had done—but I could make decisions now that would change the future. Not just for me, but for the generations who would come after me. I had allowed the enemy to convince me that I was powerless, voiceless, helpless, useless, meaningless, a victim of all that has happened to me, but now I saw that I had the power to choose freedom.

Making the Choice to Move Past Your Past

The realization at graduation of how my choices affected my future were just the beginning of my transformation. Shame had made me feel marginalized—less than, unworthy, the least. It had tempted me to feel stuck in my shame, unable to change.

Do you ever feel that way? Do you ever feel that, regardless of your efforts at forgiveness and healing, you are stuck in the same bitter patterns of behavior, repeating the same broken responses? It's not that you *want* to repeat them; you just can't find a way to move past your past.

If so, I know a story in the Bible of four lepers that will liberate you. These lepers were among the most marginalized people in their day, but despite their circumstances, they found a way to get past their past. Because of their leprosy, they were outcasts with no rights, no property, and no means of support. They weren't allowed to work, so every day they made their way to the city gate to beg for food and money (2 Kings 7:3).

At the time of this story, there was also a famine in Samaria so bad that the people were not only eating donkeys' heads but also cooking and eating their own children (2 Kings 6:28–29). I know that sounds depraved, but after all that Nick and I see traveling the globe helping rescue victims of human trafficking, I can actually wrap my mind around it. People today will literally sell one or two of their own children, sometimes in an effort to keep their other children alive. We who have never known the devastation of mass starvation cannot fathom the desperation that leads to such depravity, but it is real. It was in Samaria back then, and it is in the world today. Horrific conditions often lead to horrific actions.

But in the case of the lepers, a brave and profound action turned the tide for everyone in their part of the world, as the Syrian army besieged Samaria. The four lepers, who turned out to be quite the philosophers, asked a question—one that perhaps you should ask yourself:

> *They said to one another, "Why are we sitting here until we die? If we say, 'We will enter the city,' the famine is in the city, and we shall die there. And if we sit here, we die also. Now therefore, come, let us surrender to the army of the Syrians. If they keep us alive, we shall live; and if they kill us, we shall only die."*
>
> 2 Kings 7:3–4 NKJV

Why are we sitting here?

What practical reasoning! "If we just sit here, then there's a 100 percent chance that we will die. That's a given. If we leave this gate, start moving, and walk to the camp of the invading army—well, from the sound of things, nobody is surviving that either. So, worst-case scenario: We'll probably be captured and killed. But best-case scenario: There is maybe a 1 percent chance that we might be spared."

So they ask, "Why are we sitting here until we die?"

A key to becoming shame-free is choosing to change your perspective, because when you do, you can begin to change your posture. When you choose to focus more on what Jesus has done for you than on what others have done or said to you, you will have the faith to stand up and start moving forward. Remaining focused on your past pain, hurt, or offense will ensure you stay seated at the gate of your misery, stuck in an endless cycle of obsessive rumination.

I have learned that in order to get unhooked from the pain of my past, I have to continuously choose to change my perspective. I need to look at things through God's eyes—through the resurrection power of Jesus. He bore my shame, so his perspective is much different than mine. He is fighting for me from a place of victory, so that I might look at my future through the "resurrection lens" instead of the "shame lens." When I changed the lenses in my spiritual glasses, the future suddenly looked brighter, full of possibility, hope, and purpose instead of defeat and negativity. When I chose to change my perspective, I found that I no longer had to sit in defeat at the gate of shame, accepting this as my lot in life. I had the power to stand up and move past my past. It was a life-transforming revelation for me.

Choosing this change in perspective alters how we see everything.

- It changes "I've tried, but I can't escape the images of the abuse I suffered or the voices that have always degraded me," to "God sustained me through the abuse of my past and heals my brokenness so that I might shine as a beacon of hope to others."

- It changes "I come from a family of addictions and am doomed to repeat the family curse," to "I am the family member freed from addiction. God's work in me breaks generations of addiction and begins a new heritage of sobriety that my children and grandchildren can follow."

- It changes "I'm the child of divorce and can't trust anyone to be loyal," to "Through God's love, I'm discovering how to build trust in a relationship, and I have every hope of learning how to enjoy true intimacy."

- It changes "I've never experienced whatever 'normal' or 'healthy' or 'wholesome' or 'lovely' really is," to "I will discover what it is to be deeply known and loved and treasured."

- It changes "Over and over again I've been used and deceived," to "What the enemy meant for evil, God meant for good, and he is healing me at the deepest levels of my being."

- It changes "There is no way out of the twisted relationships in my life," or "These are the only kind of people I feel comfortable with," or "These are the only kinds of friends who will ever accept me," to "Now that I am no longer imprisoned by shame, I can become a true friend to others and choose new friends wisely."

- It changes "I'm too damaged, flawed, and beyond repair to ever experience a healthy, satisfying life," to "I'm not damaged goods, condemned to remain begging at the gate. I'm a daughter of the king, called to life-changing kingdom work."

- It changes "I tried once and failed dismally," to "I can try again because of the grace of God."
- It changes "I can't do that because I am not gifted or educated or confident," to "I can do all things through Christ who strengthens me."

It changes *everything* from fear to hope and faith. Take every fact and circumstance of your life and make the choice to see it anew through a new lens that reflects these truths:

- God has a destiny for me (Jeremiah 29:11; Psalm 37:23–24; John 15:16);
- God has a purpose for me (Psalm 139:16; Ephesians 2:10);
- God is going to use me to make a difference in the world (Philippians 1:6; 1 Corinthians 12:4–7).

When the lepers began to look through the resurrection lens instead of the shame lens, it shifted the course of their entire existence. They had spent their whole lives *sitting*. They felt tied to the gates. The gates had become their security, their source of food and sustenance. They had survived so long at the gates they didn't know how to do anything differently—but begging for food was no longer going to work.

They had not realized that they were free to choose, but they were beginning to. They began to realize that despite their shame-filled existence, they really weren't powerless. They could make some decisions. They could get moving.

They could take some first steps. Their change in perspective was changing the way they had always lived—and processed life.

Their debate sounds all too familiar to me.

Every time I've sat in front of a new gate—revealed to me by God's mercy and grace—I've had the choice to stay stuck or get to moving, just like the lepers. I've had to recognize each time that it was a new opportunity for God to heal me of more shame. It was this way when I first learned to speak in front of hundreds, and then thousands, and then tens of thousands. It was this way when I wrote *Undaunted*, then *Unstoppable*, and even *Unashamed*. It was this way when the Lord told me to start A21, and then Propel Women.

Gates can be so intimidating, because they spark our shame responses: *Who am I? What if I'm not good enough? What if I fail? Who will ever listen to me? I'm not qualified.*

The enemy will put a gate from your past in front of every new thing to which God is calling you, and you will have to decide if you will take a risk and move forward.

I can imagine some of your gates . . .

- They will laugh at me if I try to join the choir.
- My ex-husband said no one will love me, so why would I put myself out there and try to date? After all, he knows me better than anyone.
- The women's ministry numbers declined when I took over. I must not have discerned the voice of God. I must not be the right person for the job.

- If I were fully woman, I would have had children by now.

- I've been single all of my adult life. Who wants to marry a thirty-five-year-old?

- I'm younger than every employee in that department. Who am I to lead that team?

- I'm too old to make a difference. I've missed my opportunity.

- I could never go back to school to get qualified. I'm not smart enough.

- I could never trust a man again after the way I was abused.

- I lost my job and family because of my addiction. I'm clean, but who would trust me again?

We *all* have gates. Likewise, we *all* have a choice whether to stay sitting or to get up and get moving. Of all the gates I've gotten up from—and there have been more than I can count—I will never forget the one I was facing when it came to my future with Nick.

A Risk I Had to Take

Nick and I had been dating for a year, and it was clear that he was getting more serious. The emotional intimacy growing between us was something I'd never experienced with anyone before. In that time, I'd come so far in understanding God's love for me, and yet this closeness with Nick was churning to the surface all the turmoil of the sexual abuse I'd suffered—abuse I had long kept secret, hidden away.

The battle inside me was real. I was sitting at the relational gate of shame and debating my fate—to stay or move, just like the lepers. I was trying to decide whether to tell Nick everything—or not. My pain was great, and all I could do was sit there, which is exactly what the enemy wanted.

The enemy always wants us to believe that we need to stop hurting before we can move. What a lie! We must move forward even if it is painful. The freedom on the other side is what we need and want. Yes, I was still feeling a great deal of emotional pain because of the abuse—but I also knew without a doubt that the Holy Spirit was prompting me: The time had come. Hurting or not, I had to move forward. This was a choice I had to make in my journey toward freedom. I had to have the courage to tell Nick the truth. He knew I had been abused, but I had never risked saying more than a single sentence. I had never gone into any detail. I knew to be free I had to tell him the full extent of the truth. Like the lepers, I had to take a risk to gain more freedom.

What I didn't know is that God was looking out for my future marriage. God knew I would take all my baggage into my marriage—and it would have affected our intimacy, our trust, our communication, everything. I might not have realized it, but I would have made Nick pay for what others had done to me. My shame and all its damage wasn't his fault, but we would have both lived with the fruit of it. By choosing freedom, by getting it out into the light, I was removing the enemy's power to keep me bound.

The weight of the shame was so real. Whenever I was with Nick, there it was, dragging me down, shackling me with feelings of being soiled, stained, and defective, unfit to be loved by this good man. Shame's lies!

For months, I'd spent half the time wanting to share everything with Nick about my past and the other half positive that I wanted to never mention it. My thoughts swung back and forth . . .

All the hurt I'd hidden—yet still felt—for years welled up inside. I'd thought I had dealt with it, resolved it, put it to rest. But now those old wounds threatened to reopen at any moment.

So one night I told him . . . everything . . . how I had been abused for many years as a girl, by several different men. When I said the word *abused*, I started to shake. Telling the man I loved what other men had done to me was the hardest thing I had ever done.

As I spoke, I couldn't look at Nick. But I poured out what I'd kept secret for years, things that had become unspeakable to me. And once I'd breached the dam, there was no holding anything back—it came out in a flood. The things others had done to me when I was younger, and the things I had willfully chosen to do when I was older. *If I'm going to lose you over this, Nick,* I thought, *then you may as well know it all.* I held nothing back. Absolutely nothing.

Finally, I stopped. Nick had not once interrupted. I had not once looked up, and now I felt completely exposed, vulnerable, spent. And yet, though I know it sounds cliché, I also felt a great weight lifted off me. I felt a freedom I hadn't experienced before.

What I didn't understand then was that the great weight I felt lifted from my shoulders was the weight of shame that had fled now that the light of truth had been shined into all of the dark corners where it had been hiding. The freedom I suddenly felt was the freedom from shame's slavery that God had been calling me to for some time.

Nick reached out and pulled me to him and held me for the longest time. At last he said, "I'm just so sorry that this happened to you, Chris. I'm just so sorry." And he was. His words, actions, and expressions of the next few weeks confirmed it.

He hadn't pulled away. He hadn't rejected me. He had pulled me even closer!

Through Nick's love for me, God was showing me just a glimpse of the divine and infinite love he himself had for me.

I had risked being vulnerable and survived it! And it was oh so worth it! God had prepared my path. He had chosen Nick as the right road for me—the safe path to take these painful steps toward healing.

Get Up!

So I have to ask you: What gate do you now sit passively beside, constrained, unable to move in order to meet your needs? Trust me, I know there is *always* a gate.

Are you so plagued by fear and insecurity that you never risk new opportunities?

Why are you sitting there?

Maybe you've isolated yourself emotionally because of memories of abuse or embarrassment over failure. Do you tend to try to control your circumstances—and other people—so that you won't fall victim to the unexpected?

Whatever coping mechanisms you adopted to compensate for your shame, do you see yourself, today, as crippled by them—forever marked with the scars of your leprosy, reduced to an existence lingering at the gate and forever disqualified from the victorious life of making a difference in this world?

So many of us spend our whole lives sitting at this gate, believing, *Because of what happened to me in my past, because of mistakes I've made, because of the life I've led or the ways I've been victimized, I can't move. Every time I try to move on, shame drags me back to this same locked gate, doomed to just sit, impoverished and starving, shackled to that clinging shame forever. I am a shame leper, forever unclean, and there's nothing I can do to break away from it. This is who I am.* We've felt stuck for so long that we've become accustomed to just sitting here at the gate of our prison.

I was. Before Nick, I avoided dating. It was safer. Deep down, I knew what I was like. I kept my emotions so bottled up that I scared people away from me. The walls I designed to protect me actually imprisoned me.

The truth is, when you've long been crouched at the prison gates of shame, your muscles atrophy. You are cramped and locked in place. It hurts to move, let alone move forward into the unknown. But you have to, even if it hurts.

I know what it's like to do this spiritually—and physically—and both require us to endure pain to get healthy. While on a family skiing vacation years ago, I tore my ACL. The surgical procedure to repair the front of my knee required using a piece of my hamstring tendon from behind my knee. They grafted it in, using strips to secure the torn ligament. My physical therapist told me, "Christine, you will heal quickly or slowly, completely or partially, based on your willingness to embrace the pain of recovery. And sometimes, embracing that pain is more painful than the original pain of the injury."

Physically and spiritually, it's the same. We must embrace the pain of moving forward if we are to heal fully. We have to choose to get up—and trust God it will be worth the risk.

Get Moving!

The lepers risked it all. They got up and started moving. *"At dusk they got up and went to the camp of the Arameans"* (2 Kings 7:5).

This was a daring move for the lepers. Because they carried leprosy with them, they knew that they would find no welcome from anyone anywhere. They had no provisions. They were thirsty and weak from hunger. The security of the gate where they had begged for years may have been meager, but it was all they knew, and they were leaving it for the unknown. Gutsy. But they did it. They passed through their gate and went out toward the enemy camp. And when they did, a remarkable chain reaction was set in motion.

> *When they reached the edge of the camp, no one was there, for the Lord had caused the Arameans to hear the sound of chariots and horses and a great army, so that they said to one another, "Look, the king of Israel has hired the Hittite and Egyptian kings to attack us!" So they got up and fled in the dusk and abandoned their tents and their horses and donkeys. They left the camp as it was and ran for their lives.*
>
> 2 Kings 7:5–7

While the lepers had been sitting at the gate, they had no idea that God was on the move! Unbeknownst to them, God had struck fear into the hearts of the Arameans, which caused them to abandon their camp and run for their lives, leaving everything behind.

I love this part of the story because it reflects how God has, over and over again, worked in my life. Each time I have overcome my fear, overcome my shame, overcome my inertia, and made a move through the gate—even if I was so weak and in pain that I limped all the way—I have found that God has already been moving on my behalf. Just as he honored the faith of the four lepers even before they had acted on it, he has likewise honored my willingness to finally get to my feet and limp on. He honored the great risk I took in telling Nick about my deepest shame. He honored the fact I got moving!

Imagine the lepers' shock when, in fear and trembling,

they approached the enemy camp. They had most likely assumed they would be executed, but they had at least a slim hope that they might be spared and perhaps even fed. It was dusk. They probably snuck as quietly as possible to the camp's edge. And then . . .

The men who had leprosy reached the edge of the camp, entered one of the tents and ate and drank. Then they took silver, gold and clothes, and went off and hid them. They returned and entered another tent and took some things from it and hid them also.

2 Kings 7:8

Can you imagine their shock? Their delight? I can picture them, weak from starvation, grabbing by the handful the food they found in the tents, filling their mouths, savoring the flavors. I imagine them passing drinks to one another, at first gulping them hastily, water or wine dripping from parched lips down the beards that covered their emaciated necks. While they'd been sitting at the gate, starving, trying to overcome their fear, a wealth of things they needed—food and drink, silver and gold, clothing—had been waiting for them, unprotected, abandoned, and free for the taking! They gathered what they could and hid it. They were no longer poor! They had struck gold! They had a treasure.

When I chose to leave my gate of relational shame, I got more than just love and acceptance from Nick. So much more. I encountered another facet of the unconditional love of God. I realized I was truly wanted, known, chosen, and accepted, despite my past and many failings. I cannot fathom where I would be today if Jesus had not given me the grace to get up and walk across the threshold of that gate. Nick has been with me every step of the journey for the past twenty years, and I could have missed it by not choosing to move on. God has so much more for you on the other side of your gate. Your greatest days are ahead of you.

Choices Determine Destiny

The lepers found treasure and plentiful food and drink—because they exercised their freedom to choose, and they chose to get moving. And they took their newfound freedom and plenteousness a step further. They didn't hoard all the blessings they encountered—they shared them (2 Kings 7:9–11). They shared all the wealth with everyone.

Can you imagine the looks on the faces of the gatekeepers when they heard the report of such incredible news from the lepers? They knew these men. Perhaps they had even watched them stagger off toward the camp and had assumed they'd been killed by the Arameans. Now those same lepers had returned declaring that the enemy camp was deserted and that valuable goods were there for the taking.

When the king heard the news, he wanted to know exactly what had happened. Where had the Syrians gone? Was this a trap of some sort? So he sent out scouts who returned with the astounding news that, indeed, the Arameans had fled, and in their haste had left the road littered with garments and weapons (2 Kings 7:15).

Those four lepers, once sitting and starving, became the voice of freedom to an entire besieged city. Because they had dared to change their perspective and their posture, to go from passively sitting to standing and moving, they motivated an entire city to action and brought an end to everyone's starvation. That's one of the great things about freedom. Once we've tasted it, we want to go back to where we suffered and help everyone else to taste it too—to experience the same hope and provision.

I know I do. I've been set free by the love of Jesus—and I want everyone to experience his miraculous love. That's why I've written this book. That's why I travel and teach. That's why I help others gain freedom through the work of A21. That's why I reach out with Propel Women.

You too are free to choose to get up and get moving into the beautiful future God has for you. Like the lepers, you will find an abundance of riches and freedom.

God loves you unconditionally. He's waiting, eager to set you free from all shame, because there are even more women needing to hear about your freedom. So put your eyes on the road ahead and get to moving! Choices really do determine destiny—and God has given you the power to choose!

Chapter 6

THE BEAUTY OF THE WILDERNESS

I have met a woman who will take you to another country—
Greece!" fifteen-year-old Yun's mother said. "There she
will give you a job as a live-in babysitter where you will earn
much more than you do here in the factory—much more
than you can earn anywhere here in Vietnam. And your pay-
check will be sent to me every month to help us live. This is
good for you and good for your family."

Up to that point, Yun had never had the sense that anything she did or said was "good for the family."

"From the time I was a little girl in Vietnam," she recalls,
"I knew of my parents' shame and sadness that they had given
birth to a baby girl, rather than the boy they had wanted."

Yun knew the shame that can come from just being a
woman, because in her culture, a boy was more valued than
a girl—not just at birth, but for a lifetime.

When she was eleven, her father died in a work acci-
dent, and Yun was forced to work in a local factory to help
her family make ends meet. With no sense of hope for the

future, and no praise or affirmation from those whose love she craved, Yun felt worthless apart from the meager income she produced.

When Yun arrived in Greece, nothing was as her mother had promised. On her first day, she was locked in a room where her new boss brutally raped her. Then she was told that she would work as a prostitute, and that if she refused, she would be tortured and killed. Terrified, Yun did what her captors demanded. Even so, threats of death became a regular part of her life, as did the beatings she received for any "mistake" she made, or any time a client was unhappy.

Yun had become one of the 1.2 million children sold annually into sexual slavery.[1] Like most of them, Yun never again had any contact with her family. Sadly, the rest of her story is similar too.

Over the next three years, Yun was moved around to at least fifteen different brothels and strip clubs, forced to service up to thirty clients a day. She had had no dreams or hope for the future, and her disgust and shame over the things she was forced to do ate away at any remaining sense of self-worth. Even so, she discovered a tiny spark, a longing, deep inside herself: she longed for freedom.

Though held under lock and key, Yun was desperate to escape, so desperate that in spite of the threats, she risked her life in repeated attempts to flee. Each time, her captors pursued her, found her, and dragged her back into slavery, punishing her with brutal beatings and threats of an agonizing death.

The last time Yun attempted to escape, she was beaten

so badly she had to be hospitalized. When the hospital discovered that Yun did not possess the proper identification documents, they informed the police that she was in the country illegally.

Fearful of the authorities and too ashamed to admit that she was a sex slave, Yun didn't dare report her heartbreaking story. When she had recovered enough to be released from the hospital, she was taken to a detention center—again under lock and key—and scheduled for deportation. But what could possibly await her back in Vietnam? She would be a poverty-stricken, broken woman, forever soiled by years as a prostitute.

Yun saw no way out, no positive outcome. Behind her in the streets of Greece was the army of her former captors. Before her stood the threat of deportation, poverty, and shame. She felt trapped and desperate. Yun didn't know a God she could call on for miraculous deliverance.

But God knew Yun.

And God was about to deliver her.

In her city in Greece, A21 visits detention centers weekly to find women such as Yun, and it was there that our staff encountered her for the first time. One day, just a few days after Yun arrived at the detention center, a kind woman introduced herself and asked if she could interview Yun. At first, Yun was afraid to answer the woman's questions. But so unprepared was she for the woman's warmth, so unaccustomed to being treated with care and concern, that soon she was spilling her entire story.

A21 was able to get Yun's deportation orders reversed

and helped her obtain a visa so that she could legally stay in the country. We invited her to move into one of our aftercare homes where she could heal and begin a journey toward a new life, a free life.

God made a way for Yun where there was no way.

Delivered But Not Free

From the first day that eighteen-year-old Yun arrived at the A21 home, her posture and demeanor told her story of shame. As you would suspect, most of these women were tricked, kidnapped, or sold into sexual slavery. They have endured far more than physical captivity. They have been debased and degraded, humiliated beyond words, beaten into submission, and forced to endure heinous acts. By the time they step across the threshold of an A21 home, the slavery they carry with them extends far beyond bolts on doors. It has broken their hearts. It has fractured their souls and left invisible wounds beyond our knowing. It has penetrated their minds. Freedom from such internal slavery is far harder to win than physical freedom. They are held captive by shame at its very worst.

Yun behaved like all women do who enter into A21 care. Head hung low, eyes downcast, she made no eye contact with anyone, even when words of kindness and care were offered. She quietly followed as she was led to her room, lifting her eyes only enough to glance nervously at her surroundings as if waiting for some lurking danger to reveal itself. She followed others to the table for meals, but sat head down, expressionless and uncommunicative, seemingly oblivious to the overtures of friendship from staff or other residents.

When the A21 staff offered her clothes of her own, Yun shunned flattering styles and pretty colors. Unlike some of the other women in the home who had grown accustomed to dressing provocatively during their months or years in sexual slavery, believing it was the only way they'd be found worthy of attention, Yun insisted on dressing modestly in shapeless garb of dull colors. She seemed to want not only to cover up but to disappear. Even at a beach outing, she refused a swimsuit, insisting instead on shorts and a T-shirt. Yun didn't *want* people to look at her; she didn't want attention of any kind. She didn't want to stand out. Clearly, hiding in shame was deeply ingrained in Yun. Everything about her appearance and demeanor seemed to say *Let me be invisible. I am unworthy. I am ashamed.*

At the A21 home, Yun's circumstances had changed dramatically. The bolted doors were gone. Her captors were no longer brutalizing her. She was no longer forced to prostitute herself in order to survive. She was no longer a slave. But Yun was not experiencing the euphoria of freedom. One look at her made it abundantly clear—shame still held her captive. Yun had been schooled in shame, and she now carried those lessons inside her: she believed herself worthless, guilty, at fault, useless, empty, abandoned, alone, unlovable, and unloved.

Yun was delivered, but she was not yet free.

The Power of the Wilderness
to Change Us

Freedom would require a journey for Yun. It wouldn't be easy, nor would it happen overnight. She would need to follow a similar path to the one the children of Israel took when they left Egypt (Exodus 13–15). Released by the Egyptian Pharaoh, they headed out of the land of captivity in hopes of freedom, but Pharaoh later changed his mind about letting them go. He commanded his army to pursue them—all the way to the Red Sea. The Israelites had left having only known slavery all their lives. They had trusted Moses— God's leader for them—and felt trapped at the edge of the sea as Pharaoh's army chased after them.

But God instructed Moses to stretch out his hand over the water, and as he did, God miraculously parted the sea, and the Israelites crossed on dry ground. Then the sea crashed in on Pharaoh's army and drowned their enemy. The people had been delivered—saved! But were they free?

Not even close. Yes, they'd been delivered from physical slavery. But when they turned their backs to the Red Sea and looked in the direction of the Promised Land—the land God had promised them—as far as the eye could see there was nothing but desolate wilderness (Exodus 16).

The wilderness was a place filled with unknowns—but it was a land of great purpose. It was the place where the people's wilderness mentalities, the negative mindsets they developed while in captivity, would be exposed—all their wrong thoughts, attitudes, longings, and habits, all of their doubt, fear, unbelief, emptiness, and unforgiveness. But it also would be the place where God would strengthen their hearts and souls. It was where he would transform their minds so that they would no longer think like defeated slaves but like victorious free people. If they were going to overcome the walls and giants that awaited them in the Promised Land, they would need to strengthen their very damaged heart, soul, and mind muscles—to have these internal settings recalibrated.

For 430 years they had been beaten, ridiculed, mocked, scorned, treated as subhuman beings, overlooked, ignored, and discarded—all tragic experiences that definitely would cause anyone deep emotional, physical, spiritual, and psychological damage. Their broken hearts, wounded souls, and tormented minds needed to be restored, renewed, and reset in the wilderness so that they would know how to live and thrive in the Promised Land.

It is a difficult adjustment to learn to live free when you have only ever lived bound up. Slaves have an entirely different worldview and internal operating system than those people who live in freedom. The children of Israel would need to think, act, and see themselves in an entirely different way to anything they had known before if they were going to live *from victory* in the Promised Land rather than *for victory* as they had in Egypt.

Our wilderness seasons are the same. We routinely go through periods when we come out of bondage in one area only to reenter another spiritual wilderness to unlearn certain things and relearn other things on the way to our promised land. Sometimes these seasons are dramatic and all-consuming; other times they are less overwhelming but still very real. We would all love to bypass the wilderness, but I have discovered that despite our best efforts, there are no shortcuts. If we want to get to our promised land, we must go through a wilderness and, let me warn you, it is not like an afternoon commute.

We Have to Go *Through*

When I'm caught in heavy traffic, I get excited when I remember a shortcut. It's such a great feeling to jump off the interstate, hit a few side roads, and pass all those cars stalled in the rush-hour standstill.

But many times my brilliant idea is thwarted by highway engineers. My ingenious shortcut is suddenly sabotaged by construction, a roadblock, and then a detour that leads me through multiple turns right back to the interstate. I end up back where I started, forced to return to the traffic jam and go through it to get home.

It's the same journey on our way to our promised land. Despite our best efforts to find alternate routes, there's only one way to get there—through.

And we can go through one of two ways—in the rideshare lane that just zips along, or hugging the shoulder creeping along. We actually do have a choice about that part. Even the children of Israel could have shaved some serious time off their trip. Going through was essential for them, but their trek through the wilderness was actually only an eleven-day journey. It didn't have to take forty years, but in essence they chose that for themselves by fighting the process—grumbling, complaining, resisting the work God wanted to do *in* them.

We all have some version of the wilderness to go through. It's a season that exposes how vulnerable we are, how defenseless we feel, how small we are in comparison to the wide expanse of this world. It's how God prepares us to be well able to overcome the giants in our lives. It's a place we cycle through over and over again in our lives—but in different areas—always getting freer and freer from shame each time. It is no unexpected detour, no wrong turn, no mistake in navigation. It is the path to freedom God has chosen.

But it's never a place we go looking for. When we find ourselves there, we tend to use words like *being thrust into*, or *lost in*, or *wandering through* the wilderness. But God is changing our thinking. He is leading, transforming, delivering, and freeing us. We just have to decide that where he leads, we will follow.

God's goal for us is freedom, true spiritual freedom—a life no longer bound by the weights of shame's false guilt and relentless regret, no longer haunted by shame's fears and worries, no longer captive to shame's old habits and self-protective responses that keep us repeating those same old shame-filled patterns.

God's goal for us is not merely to change our *circumstances*—it is to change *us!* That is the evidence of his unconditional love for you and me. That was the evidence of his unconditional love for Yun.

Free From the Slavery of Shame

Yun, like many of the women rescued from trafficking, found herself *bewildered* and *unsettled* as she tried to adjust to life in the safe house—two words that capture well what a wilderness experience is like for any of us.

They certainly capture the essence of all my own wilderness experiences. They are times when I feel confused, uncertain of where I seem to be unexpectedly headed or why; the times of suffering, of hurt and loss; of feeling vulnerable or afraid; of facing unpleasant, uncomfortable, or downright painful experiences. I now know that the only way to get to the promised land of freedom is to walk through the wilderness and to embrace the pain of recovery as a part of the healing process.

Yun's journey through the wilderness was to overcome the terror that someone would take her again and hurt her more. She had to learn again how to trust people, especially authority figures. She had to forgive—her family, the traffickers, the men who violated her. She had to overcome anger—and all of the emotion from such a sense of powerlessness. And the resentment—against people and systems.

Yun had endured so much shame. She certainly did not ask for the tragic things she had endured, but many things happen to us in this fallen world that we don't deserve, ask for, or desire. She had huge struggles ahead of her, but I knew that the same God who set me free would set her free. I knew that the same God who called me daughter had called her daughter too. I knew that one day God would use all of the horrible things she'd experienced and work them together for good (Romans 8:28)—just as he had done for me. I had seen it often enough to know it was true, but I also knew she would have to commit to the process and go through her wilderness journey.

Everything she would have to overcome—like all of us—would be directly related to her experiences—not only the ones she endured as a sex slave, but also those dating back to her childhood when she felt ashamed of the fact that she was born a girl and not a boy.

Though we have all had different experiences, we share common challenges in our wilderness journey when everything familiar and secure is stripped from us. We may have been delivered from our shameful experiences, but until we learn to trust God in the wilderness by exposing our baggage and allowing him to heal our broken places, we will never experience true freedom. We will continue to hide behind the defense mechanisms we have developed that have empowered us to survive. Mechanisms such as never getting too close to anyone so we cannot be hurt, rejected, or abandoned again. Or performing for acceptance, trying to earn love and approval by pleasing people, perfectionism (my specialty), escaping through various addictions, or hiding and minimizing who we really are. We all have a list to overcome, and the wilderness is where we overcome. God leads us there to bring us out of hiding and to prepare us for what he's prepared for us. He leads us there to free us.

Remember, *"It is for freedom that Christ has set us free"* (Galatians 5:1a).

God knows what he is doing.

There's a huge difference between taking a slave out of slavery and taking the slavery out of the slave.

Taking the slave out of slavery is a *rescue mission.*

Taking the slavery out of the slave is a *preparation process.*

And the preparation process takes place in the wilderness—the land of transformation.

More than once the children of Israel lost focus of how bad life had been when they had been in bondage—enslaved—and they wanted to turn back to Egypt.

> *That night all the members of the community raised their voices and wept aloud. All the Israelites grumbled against Moses and Aaron, and the whole assembly said to them, "If only we had died in Egypt! Or in this wilderness! Why is the Lord bringing us to this land only to let us fall by the sword? Our wives and children will be taken as plunder. Wouldn't it be better for us to go back to Egypt?" And they said to each other, "We should choose a leader and go back to Egypt."*
>
> Numbers 14:1–4

How quickly we forget—when the wilderness feels too dark, too hard, too long. When we're challenged with the season of uncertainty and the process of being made stronger so we can fight the giants ahead. There are times when we forget how hard shame-filled living is, and we're tempted to yearn for what was familiar—to go back to our old ways. So we yield to the pressure.

We decide it's time to open a bottle when an unforeseen disappointment surprises us, rather than call that person who's willingly committed to helping us stay on course. Or, we answer that call we know we shouldn't, and say yes to going out with the abusive boyfriend one more time—even when all of the warning lights are flashing on the dashboard of our hearts. Or, we grow tired of the discipline of believing what God's Word says we are over the lies of mean people who have always said, "You're just a loser—and you'll always be a loser."

No matter how bad our past, it's always easier to default to our old behaviors than to keep forging new ones. So many young girls trafficked like Yun return to slavery because they cannot cope with freedom and the process of the wilderness season. So many of us struggle with the same temptations. But there is no drive-through breakthrough. We all must go through the wilderness to get to freedom so we are strong enough to defeat the giants who fuel our shame.

Jesus died to secure our freedom—freedom from sin, freedom from death, freedom to live once again as Adam and Eve lived—in the garden—unashamed, having daily fellowship with our loving Creator and each other. In heaven we will fully enjoy that ultimate freedom. But we don't have to wait to walk in freedom: Jesus offers us freedom from sin's slavery *now*. He does not want us burdened by it *here*, *on earth.* Look at the rest of that verse in Galatians: *"Stand firm, then, and do not let yourselves be burdened again by a yoke of slavery"* (Galatians 5:1b).

Jesus died not only to give us *life insurance* for when we die but *life assurance* here on earth *today.* Jesus came not only for us to drop our shame-filled life but also to lead us into a shame-free life. He came that we might have life and life more abundantly (John 10:10). Free to walk into the fullness of every promise that he has for our lives. Free to be who he made us to be. Free to do all that he created us to do.

From Deliverance to Freedom

Though Yun was free physically, she had no idea who she was in Christ. So A21's goal for Yun included God's healing and freedom—physically, emotionally, and psychologically. We taught her that different issues will arise at different times in her life as Jesus leads her into her freedom more fully. He does not deal with everything at once because we wouldn't be able to bear it. He is gentle and kind, tenderhearted and patient. He knows it takes a lifetime for his image to be forged in us, for us to learn to walk out the shame-free life he has provided.

Today, Yun has the tools to know how to navigate her future because she has walked through the initial phase of her healing process—the part of the wilderness that is always the most significant and life-transforming. She has been taught how to embrace the gift of the wilderness and to recognize there will always be wilderness experiences as God continues to shape us into the true image bearers he created us to be. She knows those wilderness experiences always will be defined as trials, temptations, or difficult challenges.

And she understands the wilderness's purpose: It's the place where our baggage is exposed, *so that* we can drop our baggage, *in order to* pick up the freedom God has for us. It's how we move on from just being delivered to truly being free. Free to be strong enough to face our walls and fight the giants we will encounter in our promised land.

That was what it was for me—the first time and every time since.

God has taken me through the wilderness again and again. In fact, the day I made the decision to truly follow Jesus on that balcony in Zurich, I left my own spiritual Egypt and began the journey to healing and wholeness, my promised land. There is no doubt that this was the single most difficult wilderness journey of my life. I walked away from my destructive lifestyle and unhealthy relationships toward my future purpose. I left everything that was familiar to embrace the unknown. I was exhilarated and terrified simultaneously. I expected that once I'd left my old life and joined God's team, I would feel free and could simply forget the past and move on. But I didn't. The blood of Jesus did not give me amnesia. I was forgiven and had access to all of the promises of God in Christ Jesus, but I still carried a broken heart, a wounded soul, and a tormented mind—because slavery destroys our internal settings.

I needed a hard reset to bring my heart, soul, and mind

into alignment with God's Word. I was delivered from my past, but I still had to learn to step into the freedom of my future. The lessons I learned back then and the skills I developed in those wilderness years, I continue to use today. There is probably nothing more important I can share with you than the lessons in the next two chapters because I continue to apply these principles daily in my life. I have never gone through a wilderness period as dramatic as I did back then, but I must maintain a vigilant commitment to continue to strengthen these muscles daily if I am to continue to possess more of the promised land that Jesus has for me.

Chapter 7

GOD MOVES IN SO
WE CAN MOVE ON

W hen I was thirty, I had just become the state director of a ministry called Youth Alive in New South Wales, Australia. Though I was thriving in so many areas, God knew that this was perfect timing for me to deal with more of my damaged heart, soul, and mind. Out of his great love, grace, and mercy for me, he was looking out for my future.

Our office was in Sydney, and I was leading a staff in youth outreach and ministry events all over the state. I was busy traveling, teaching, and running seminars in schools and communities. Plus we were holding large-scale youth rallies in arenas. It was a whirlwind. I was living the dream!

But not wanting to disappoint anyone, especially God who had given me this opportunity, I was seriously over-committed. I was running so hard, I didn't have much time to process things with my team. I knew they were as passionate as I was, loyal and faithful, so I just kept going faster, and expected them to keep up. There was so much fruit, so many were being helped, and God was using my past to bring freedom to so many young people.

I had just come back from a trip, excited about all God was doing, the day Joanna knocked on my door. She was a dedicated member of my staff, responsible for organizing many of the details of our outreach events. She was conscientious, hardworking, and warmhearted.

"Do you have time to talk?" she asked.

I greeted her and motioned her in, trying to sound positive—but in truth, anxiety surged through me. I could tell by the tone of Joanna's voice and the look on her face—brows furrowed, eyes troubled—that she was uneasy. *What's wrong? What if there's a conflict that needs to be resolved? Is she or someone else angry at me? Did I do something wrong?* I was afraid. I hated confrontation and conflict. Was I about to find myself thrust into them? I wasn't yet fully aware of shame's influence on my life, so when shame's whispers came sweeping into my mind, I didn't yet recognize the enemy at work.

I wanted to appear confident and in control, even though I felt just the opposite. Shame is an expert at hiding, remember? And I had an advanced degree in it!

Yes, she knew that we were running hard, she said. She knew that I was a woman on a mission, gifted, anointed, and focused. She knew that God was doing amazing things.

"But I just can't keep up," she said. "I feel like I've been disappointing you in so many ways. I can't bear failing you any longer. So after much consideration, I've decided that it would be best for me to resign."

I stared back in stunned silence. Joanna was one of my core leaders! I relied on her immensely. I hadn't seen this coming. She was quitting? That was bad enough. But even worse was her reason: her sense that she was *repeatedly failing me.*

She poured out her heart—words of explanation and pain that I had never before heard, words that painted a picture of her experience under my leadership. It was not a pretty picture. She described unrealistic deadlines for her and my staff. She described my pushing for impossible performance standards. She gave examples of my being short-tempered at times in order to get a desired result, as if I were more concerned with results than I was with their well-being. She told me of her long hours, her tremendous efforts to do her very best—yet no matter how hard she worked, how much effort she applied, it seemed it was never enough.

And there they were—the telling words. "Never enough." My shame buttons were all being simultaneously pressed: the rejection button, the perfectionist button, the "not-good-enough" button. A lifetime of shame-induced self-defense mechanisms sprang into action, without me even recognizing them.

I felt my face burning as shame shouted silently: *Bad leader, critical leader, demanding leader! Perfectionist! You're the one who's not good enough! They'll probably all quit now. Who would want to work with you? You're failing at this just as you've failed at so many other things.* I wanted to run for cover. I took her comments as a personal rejection.

So what did I do? I began to defend myself. And to make matters worse, I even began to justify myself with regard to some of her specific examples, pointing out where she *had* fallen short, so I'd *had* to correct her and hold her accountable, for the sake of the ministry. After all, that was my job as the leader, right?

In tears, Joanna didn't try to defend herself. Instead, she listened. Sadly, my response was proving her point, though I didn't realize it at the time. I was driven by performance, satisfied with nothing but perfection, and I imposed criticism and blame when those impossible standards weren't met. But God bless that dear young woman. In spite of my defensive reaction, through her tears Joanna found the courage to tell me what I needed to hear.

I was devastated. I'd had no idea that this blind spot existed. (That's why it's called a *blind* spot!) My external world was flourishing, but I needed internal work. I took off that afternoon and went on a prayer walk with Jesus. Although I didn't realize it at the time, this was the *beginning* of a process to discover some lingering residue of my past, residue that if not dealt with would hinder my future in the promised land. I faced a choice: I could see this either as shame or as an opportunity to be further healed and conformed to his image—and walk through a new wilderness experience.

I find that the wilderness can hit us in the most unexpected times—like when we think we're flourishing, and so is everyone around us. Sometimes we do not see where we are still broken or damaged or living a shame-filled life.

That conversation with Joanna was a major turning point for me. It started me on a path of healing and prompted me to seek help through mentoring and accountability. I began the hard work of recognizing and addressing deeply broken areas in myself.

God had exposed my weakness, my need for growth. He had opened my eyes to see that my performance-driven nature was a by-product of my own unmet needs, my own brokenness. I was carrying shame's baggage into ministry with me—in this case, perfectionism, control, isolation, and a hard heart. It was time to drop that baggage. Only then would my heart be softened so that my arms could embrace others in our *mutual* lack of perfection and control. I was a gifted leader, but a wounded one, and if I didn't deal with that, I would leave a wide trail of destruction behind me.

To this day, I am grateful for this courageous young woman who came to me in love and gentle honesty. She didn't expose me in front of others or humiliate me with accusations or condemnation. She came to me privately and focused on her own limitations, not my shortcomings. Clearly, she had prayed over this encounter and had sought God's guidance. Jesus was there with us, at work, at that very moment.

There is a place of divine tension between where we've been set free from shame and are flourishing, and where we are still being freed from shame and harboring it inside. While God sees this transition zone of simultaneously living in freedom and still dealing with unresolved issues as perfectly normal—something he wants us to embrace—we often wrestle with it emotionally. We feel condemned and confused, and try to cover up those vulnerable feelings and broken places with a multitude of shame-filled responses—all of which are especially exposed through our relationships with other people.

For those of us who are married, our responses hinder healthy marital communication. For those who are single, they hinder our capacity to allow people to get close to us. For those of us who have children, it impacts our parenting.

For those of us who struggle in friendships, it impacts our ability to accept others as they are, or our ability to be vulnerable and open, or our ability to believe we are truly loved—or to allow others to be themselves rather than resorting to manipulation in our attempt to control circumstances or outcomes.

For those of us building careers, it affects our ability to risk and stretch and therefore to achieve. Though my career landed in ministry, the stretching to be a shame-free leader is just as real as for someone in the corporate world.

God uses events, circumstances, and people such as Joanna to reveal areas where we are not whole, so he can bring healing and prepare us for whatever is next in his plan. He uses different situations in different seasons in the sanctification process, increasingly freeing us from shame. And he does it so that we might learn to receive love and completely love as he does.

Sure, we try to love him, but love from a broken heart is broken love. Love from a wounded soul is wounded love. Love from a tormented mind is tormented love. And this affects not only how we love God but how we love ourselves and our neighbor. As long as shame has a grip on our lives, to put it bluntly, our love is a mess!

But don't despair—which is so easy to do in the wilderness! We are being re-created by God in the image of Jesus Christ, so that we will be able to fulfill the destiny God has prepared for us. If we work with God in our wilderness, he will use it to expose where our hearts are broken, where our souls are wounded, and where our minds are tormented—and he will heal us. Not only will he expose our brokenness—our wilderness mentalities—he will pour his wholeness into it.

Jesus heals our broken hearts.

Jesus binds our wounded souls.

Jesus renews our tormented minds.

He did it with me, and he can do it for you.

Jesus Heals Our Broken Hearts

The physical heart muscle, fed by arteries, pumps and regulates the blood flow that carries oxygen and nutrients throughout our bodies. If we exercise that muscle through cardiovascular workouts and feed it healthy nutrients, it grows stronger. But let it languish and feed it toxins, and we all know what happens: the muscle grows weak and the arteries get clogged.

The same is true of our spiritual hearts. The heart is the seat of our passions; it drives and compels us to be who we are and act as we do. It is the essence of our character. So what happens if our spiritual heart is fed toxins and we let it languish? It too grows weak, gets clogged, and sends those poisonous toxins pumping through our lives. When shame has been pumping through a heart, over time the heart itself grows toxic. When we are wounded, we leak toxic waste, and that waste poisons us and the people around us—even when we are completely unaware of it—just like I did with Joanna. The reality is:

- Hurt people hurt people.
- Broken people break people.
- Shattered people shatter people.
- Damaged people damage people.
- Wounded people wound people.
- Bound people bind people.

Many of us have been hurt, suffered offense, and then lived with it unforgiven in our lives. All of my shame-filled brokenness and patterns of behavior were hurting my staff at Youth Alive, but I didn't know it. Sometimes we have experienced so much abandonment and rejection that we choose flawed defense mechanisms to try to soothe those broken places in our lives.

And sometimes we have damaged hearts and don't even know why. When I was thirty-three years old, I discovered my brother and I were adopted. It was shocking. Surreal.

Weeks later, when I saw my actual, original birth certificate, it stated I was "unnamed" and "unwanted." You can read this story in my book *Undaunted*, but what I want you to think about now is how that affected me even though I was unaware of it for three decades. Adopted. Unwanted. Unnamed.

I had suffered from such rejection in my childhood—and it had been there from the beginning. Even before the beginning!

Over time, I learned that my biological mother wasn't married when she became pregnant with me—and conceiving a child out of wedlock was shameful for a Greek woman in the 1960s. So I was conceived in shame, left in a hospital in shame, and then adopted in shame.

My adopted mom and dad suffered the shame of not being able to conceive . . . it was looked down upon culturally . . . so after years of trying, they adopted my older brother and me—and later were able to have my younger brother naturally. But because of social stigmas, they kept it hush about us older two. Yes, they loved us before we were born, and couldn't wait until our birth mothers delivered so they could hold us and love us . . . but their shame and our shame—and my birth mother's shame—all wrapped up together was more than a heart can process and be healthy. It can't help but be damaged.

I know what it is to find all sorts of toxins clogging my heart and pumping through my life. I was that way in my first years of faith. I had suffered so much abuse and carried so much shame that my heart was choked with perfectionism, unforgiveness, bitterness, guilt, and anger—and I was taking it out unknowingly on Joanna and the rest of my team. When we carry toxins within us, no matter how hard we try, we still leak them, infecting those around us, ultimately destroying the relationships we value.

I'll never forget how I sat there listening to Joanna, trying to remain calm and Christlike, as all the while my many shame buttons were being pushed at once! My fragile self-esteem took a sudden plunge. Though I tried at first to be understanding, deep down I grew angry, hurt, and full of pain. Like Adam and Eve in the garden, I went from guilt (blaming myself) to shame (defending myself) to blame (correcting Joanna as though she was at fault).

All of these responses are the inevitable by-products of shame, but when we're bound by shame, we might not even realize that our reactions are shame-based. I knew that God had a great purpose and destiny for my life, and oh, how I wanted to step into that! When I began working hard in youth ministry, full steam ahead, I wanted to change lives and change the world for Jesus. But there was a disparity—a vast gap—between what I wanted to do and be and what was going on in my *inner* world.

This, I believe, is where so many of us who suffer from shame get stuck in the wilderness! We feel that painful gap between what we know *should* be going on inside of us—love, forgiveness, kindness, joy, patience, peace, and so on—and what is *actually* going on inside of us—anger, blame, impatience, jealousy, turmoil, judgment, suspicion, and so on.

After Joanna came to me, I got personal with God. I talked with him about my scariest, ugliest thoughts, feelings, and memories. I chose to be vulnerable—something shame teaches us not to do—and seek counsel and accountability from seasoned, trustworthy mentors. When I did, God *began* to cut through my thick, hardened defense mechanisms. I began moving from deliverance to freedom in this area—from the wilderness to the promised land.

But none of this was easy. It's difficult to allow God to cut out defense mechanisms that have been clogging our hearts. After all, they have been a source of protection. We put them there for a purpose. I remember how at one point I tried to shut Nick out of my life, out of fear that no one could possibly love me if he or she knew how bad I was on the inside.

How many times do we shut people out of our lives because our defense mechanisms are trying to protect our hearts?

But as I allowed the Lord to heal my heart, my faith, strength, and courage rose. I turned from constantly trying to protect myself by controlling every detail of my life, to giving myself over to the Lord, bit by bit. A supernatural, divine exchange was occurring. God was replacing my clogged heart with his heart of flesh, because healthy hearts create healthy and fruitful lives (Ezekiel 36:26).

That exchange began subtly. But over time I grew from a person with a wounded heart to one who began to have a capacity to help others. After all, only free people can truly free people. Yes . . .

- Hurt people hurt people, *but helped people help people.*
- Broken people break people, *but rebuilt people build people.*

- Shattered people shatter people, *but whole people restore people.*
- Damaged people damage people, *but loved people love people.*
- Wounded people wound people, *but healed people bind up wounds.*
- Bound people bind people, *but freed people lead others to freedom.*

I will always be grateful to Joanna for confronting me that day. How could I be the leader I am today if she hadn't been so honest? How could I lead the teams I do had she not allowed God to use her in my life? My choice to allow God to change me then is a large reason why I am leading a global ministry now.

God Binds Our Wounded Souls

I was gifted and had a capacity to minister, but because my heart was clogged and my soul was wounded, I was co-laboring with God in order to gain acceptance and approval. However, I was beginning to understand that while God did not want me to stop doing good works, I needed to allow him to change my motivation for doing them. When it rose up in my heart to be a God-worker on that balcony in Switzerland, God was leading me. But he intended all along to lead me further than I realized—all the way through a wilderness experience so that I could be healed in my heart and soul and enter into my promised land.

I needed to allow him to come into those innermost recesses of my wounded soul where, as a little girl, I had made vows such as, "I will never trust like that again. I will never open myself up to that risk again. No one will ever do that to me again." With each one of those vows, I had locked God out of the very places that he needed to enter, places filled with darkness that needed his light, life, hope, healing, and restoration.

The apostle John writes, *"Beloved, I pray that in every way you may succeed and prosper and be in good health [physically], just as [I know] your soul prospers [spiritually]"* (3 John 2 AMP). A prosperous soul is so vital. *To prosper* means to become active and strong, to thrive and flourish.

God used John 1:14 to help me understand how he was at work binding up my wounded soul with his presence. I particularly love *The Message* translation that says it so beautifully: *"The Word became flesh . . . and moved into the neighborhood."*

I love that! God moved into *my* neighborhood!

When God moves in and you give him full access to your soul, he heals your soul with his presence and allows it to flourish. *When God moves in, we move on.* Because we're able to. Without him, we cannot do it. We will inevitably become weary and run out of steam. It is God's power that is made perfect in our weakness, not our own. The key to moving from a damaged, shame-filled life to a whole, shame-free life is allowing the healing power of the love of God to permeate every crevice of our wounded soul and bring healing, wholeness, and strength.

What a contrast—it's not about *our doing more for God*; it's about giving God more access so *he can do more in us. It is only when God does more in us that he can do more through us.*

This was a massive, revolutionary concept for me. It was my true introduction to grace—not just the grace that saved me but the grace that enabled me to be free and live an abundant life. It's the grace that enabled me to move toward fulfilling my purpose.

If our soul is not open territory for the ever-expanding presence of God, we will default to the tired old yo-yo Christian behavior—three days good, two weeks bad, two months good, six weeks bad, earn some God-points with good works, lose them with wrong behavior. And where does that leave you? With fatigue, unsatisfying exhaustion, busyness, emptiness—and finally the realization that it has brought you no closer to God at all. But allow God to move in and inhabit your soul—to get into the core of that area no matter how secret and locked down—and he will strengthen and heal you.

Remember: Shame loves silence. It grows in secret. The secrets we keep about our shame, or about the things that caused it, only intensify our shame. Keep shame a secret, and it festers. It thrives in the dark where our enemy lurks, wanting to keep us immobilized. We need to let God's light shine in those places.

For those of us recovering from shame, so much of our wounded will and emotions come spilling out as behaviors to compensate for what happened in our past. For me, it was a lack of trust and a need for hyper-control. Rather than risk being abused or hurt again, I was determined to be self-sufficient and self-protective. I became the uber-achiever, so in control of my life and circumstances that I'd never need to be vulnerable to the pain of such abuse and violation again.

What is it for you?

What part of your soul do you have hidden away in a double-padlocked impenetrable safe?

- Shutting down in your marriage?
- Giving your husband the silent treatment?
- Medicating the pain with prescription drugs?
- Becoming critical of other people?
- Being overly compliant, and living in denial?
- Avoiding close friendships to remain in hiding?
- Remaining on the treadmill of performing for approval?

What destructive behaviors and patterns do you keep repeating?

- Dating anyone and everyone like crazy?
- Lashing out at your children?
- Watching TV endlessly?
- Eating uncontrollably?
- Spending arbitrarily?

What do you keep striving to achieve to soothe your wounded soul?

- Competing with your colleagues?
- Secretly celebrating when friends "get what they deserve"?

Invite God to move into those deep places so that you can move past your past, so that you can overcome the giants who produce shame in your life. Dare to give him full access.

I did. Thanks to Joanna. Because of her boldness and courage, I found a way to give the Holy Spirit the key to the locked away places in my soul—so I could maximize the gifts and capacity he'd placed inside of me. I learned to quit performing, enjoy his presence, and let him minister through me so he could genuinely use me.

I began to be able to love Jesus with all my heart and all my soul, yet I still had a long way to go because I had spent my whole life thinking the wrong thoughts. The transformation of my heart and soul were changing the course of my life and removing my shame, but in order to walk in true freedom, my mind needed to be healed as well. As we're about to discover, there's nothing as powerful as a mind that has been healed and renewed.

Chapter 8

HE HEALED
MY MIND

W hen I was a university student, I caught the train every
morning at 7:30 a.m. from Seven Hills station in the
western suburbs of Sydney where I lived, to Redfern station
in the center of Sydney where my campus was located. The
commute took forty-five minutes, and I was grateful for
each one as I normally caught up on my assignments during
this time.

One particular morning I was running late and had a lot
on my mind because of an important exam that day. When
I got to the top of the stairs leading to the various platforms,
I skipped one habitual step: checking the destination board
for delays or platform changes. I heard a train pull up to
platform 4, and immediately rushed down the stairs and
jumped on board as the doors closed. *Just made it*, I thought,
and relaxed into a seat.

As the train pulled out of the station, I immediately
saw it was not headed toward downtown Sydney. In fact,
it was going in the exact opposite direction—toward the

mountains. I began to panic as the train picked up speed and an announcement came over the loudspeaker telling us to enjoy the ride on the express train to Katoomba, the beautiful Blue Mountains. I felt sick as I realized that I could not get off this train. I was going to miss my exam, and I had no idea when there would be another train scheduled to take me back to where I started out my journey this morning. It was the longest ride I've ever taken . . . to the wrong destination.

When the train stopped, I rose, still numb from my mistake. When the doors opened I stepped onto the platform—and moaned aloud, "How did I get here?"

The stationmaster happened to be standing nearby. He looked at me with a grin and said, "Well, young lady, you got on the wrong train, didn't you?"

It was that simple. I did not check the destination at Seven Hills station, boarded the wrong train on platform 4, and ended up in Katoomba instead of downtown Sydney. I had gotten on the wrong train and ended up at the wrong place.

Isn't that exactly our experience at the end of many days? We look around at where we ended up mentally and wonder, "God, how did I get here?"

We're angry again. Frustrated again. Lonely again. Disillusioned again. Heartbroken again. Anxious again. Hurt again. Defeated again. Fearful again.

I sometimes imagine that God wants to say to us, "Well, young lady, you just got on the wrong train of thought, didn't you?"

Our thoughts, like a train, take us somewhere.

I've discovered that if I do not manage where I want

my thoughts to take me on a daily basis, then I will end up jumping on any train of thought, often ending up where I do not want to be. I've found that, like a bullet train, I can quickly go from shame-free to shame-filled thinking.

And I don't just mean every day.

I mean *every hour of every day.*

Why?

Because I have the wrong trains of thought pulling into my mind on a regular basis. As noted in an earlier chapter, our tormented minds need healing if we're to love the Lord our God with all our heart, soul, and mind (Luke 10:27). If I do not make up my mind ahead of time that I am going to refuse to board the wrong train of thought, then I will end up at a place in my head where I do not want to be.

One of the most important lessons I have discovered is that nothing is as powerful as a mind made up. A mind made up ahead of time has the power to control the way your day goes, the way your life goes. You have the power to control who you become, because you are literally what you think—whether you choose to learn how to consciously control that or not. Proverbs 23:7 says, *"For as he thinks in his heart, so is he"* (AMP).

How crucial then for us to manage our minds. If we don't, our minds will manage us. This has been an ongoing battle for me in my journey from shame-filled to shame-free living, and it will likely be for you as well. If we disregard the destination board and jump on any train, we'll go anywhere. But if we carefully choose the train we really want to be on, we'll only go there—and that's what we want to learn to do.

Manage Your Mind

Those of us with a history of shame are at the top of the enemy's hit list for waging war on our minds and derailing our very lives. But God has a solution. Unlike the express train I was trapped on that day, we can get off the wrong train of thought at any point on the journey—by pushing the emergency stop button and choosing to board a different train of thought. And the way we learn to do this is by renewing our tormented mind. Renewing your mind empowers you to be the one managing your mind—and it brings peace. It brings healing. God reveals this transforming power in Romans 12:1–2:

> *Therefore, I **urge you,** brothers and sisters, in view of God's mercy, to offer your bodies as a living sacrifice, holy and pleasing to God—this is your true and proper worship. **Do not conform** to the pattern of this world, but **be transformed by the renewing of your mind.** Then you will be able to **test and approve** what God's will is—his good, pleasing and perfect will.* (emphasis added)

Even when I turned my life over to Christ, I didn't know anything differently than to believe the lies and accusations the enemy suggested in my mind. I had no idea what God said or thought about me—that I was fully loved, fully known, and fully accepted—because I had been listening to the enemy whisper lies to me my entire life—lies that limited my life and weren't based in truth. That's what he does. He makes up lies and spreads them nonstop. I heard a constant barrage of, "You can't, you won't, you'll never be," or, "You'll always be . . . "

Our wounds of worthlessness are constantly chafed by these accusations and never allowed to heal because we believe them and repeat them to ourselves. We hear these shame-filled thoughts in our marriages, our mothering, our friendships, at work, and as daughters, even if no one else is speaking them aloud.[1]

Because I never knew all those thoughts were lies, I jumped on those trains without ever giving any of them a second thought. I never questioned what rolled through my mind—*No one will ever love you. You're a failure. You're damaged goods. You blew it big-time.* I never asked myself: *Who sent that train—God or the enemy? Where will that train take me—into God's mind and will and purpose, or into shame—the enemy's mind, will, and purpose?*

Satan is the father of lies and the accuser of us all. When he lies, he speaks his native tongue. That's right, his native language is lying (John 8:44)! He doesn't know how to speak anything but lies . . . and for years, I didn't know how to do anything but believe those lies.

Wherever my mind went, all of my emotions and feelings followed uncontrollably—like a runaway train. "Not smart enough, fit enough, pretty enough, thin enough, good enough, holy enough."

Never enough.

Of anything.

Just as God had begun to heal my broken heart and bind my wounded soul, he began renewing my mind with his truth.

By attending church regularly, joining a Bible study group, and becoming a part of a community of Christ-followers, I eventually learned that not everyone thought the same way as I thought, especially God. In fact, the more I studied the Bible, the more I realized that my thoughts about myself and so many areas in my life were about as far away from God's thoughts as I was when I ended up in Katoomba instead of Redfern.

It was life-changing for me when I realized that I should not believe all my feelings and thoughts—especially when they contradicted the Word of God, which is the absolute truth. As Jesus said: *"If you hold to my teaching, you are really my disciples. Then you will know the truth, and the truth will set you free"* (John 8:31–32).

Knowing the truth can profoundly impact how we process the facts of our circumstances. Remember that day I found out I was adopted? The realization that I was not who I thought I was shocked me beyond words, but even though my understanding of the facts about my history changed that day, the truth never changed. God knew about my adoption all along; he had still knit me together in my mother's womb; he had a plan, purpose, and destiny for my life. A change of "facts" on my end did not change the truth about who I was from his end.

My birth certificate states the fact that I am UNNAMED child number 2508 of 1966, but the Word of God states the truth that from the womb of my mother he has named my name (Isaiah 49:1). The facts can change, but the truth has the power to change things. When my mother told me I was adopted, I made a decision in that moment to stay on the train of thought based on the truth. It was one of the single most defining moments of my life. This one decision and an ongoing commitment to stay on the train of thought based on truth of God's Word has saved me years of turmoil and torment. I renewed my mind by replacing my thoughts about myself with God's thoughts about me. I learned that I could control what thoughts I jumped on and which ones I did not. You can too.

We have to mature in choosing our thoughts. I know all of this is a tall order for our minds that have spent years tormented by shame—years of hearing and responding to the voice of shame making accusations against us. Years of shame-induced thinking that we were broken or a failure. That there is something wrong with us. That we always mess up. Thoughts that cause us to become perfectionists and people pleasers, or to be overly hard on ourselves. Years of fighting for our own significance.

But as always, God doesn't leave us alone to fight such battles. He gave us his Word. He gave us the power to exchange the enemy's lies—and everything anyone else has ever said about us—for his truth.

So how exactly do we exchange our shame-induced thinking for God's thoughts? How do we know the truth and that truth will set us free?

We begin by setting our minds at the start of every day.

Set Your Course

The devil is ever so crafty in communicating negative messages. He will do everything in his power to keep us from getting on the right train of thought. He'll bombard our thoughts because he knows that most people don't even think about what they are thinking about. He knows they will believe any lie he tells, that they will think any thought that comes to their minds.

So we have to be committed to know, to learn, and to retrain our thinking. We have to work at believing God's voice spoken through his Word, more than all the other voices that have spoken into our lives—including our own.

Begin every day by first checking the destination board and picking the right train of thoughts. Ask yourself *Where do I want to end up today?* and then set your course going in the right direction. Take God's thoughts and replace yours with his. This is the process of renewing your mind—of becoming someone who thinks, and consequently, lives differently than you do now.

I start every morning filling my mind with the Word of God. I need to remind myself of what God says about me and every circumstance in life. When I am armed with the truth of his Word, I am able to contend with the onslaught of fear, doubt, insecurity, negativity, and lies that the enemy hurls at me daily.

If this sounds like a lot of work, consider it this way: If you needed kidney dialysis every day to stay alive, you would do it, right? If you needed a pill every day to keep you alive, you would take it. I urge you to consider it that important to study the Word. The Word will keep you on track and help you to flourish in life.

Knowing who we are in Christ, and what we have in Christ, is the key to setting our course and staying on track every day. We have to think God's truth and say it daily—because it is only the truth we *know* that sets us free. And the only way to know God's Word is to read it, meditate on it, study and apply it to our everyday lives. Renewing your mind is applying the Word in a very practical way. It's changing your thoughts—the seat of power that directs your entire life, and the way it goes.

And if you're not sure what to say—if you don't know which train will take you there—you don't have to just stand around waiting and hoping for that train of thought to pull up. You can go *looking* for it—in the Word of God. Use all the tools available to us today. There are scores of different translations and versions, accessible in a variety of print editions, on the Internet, via your smartphone, or on TV or DVD, or in countless books that provide a variety of helps—and that's just the beginning. God is serious about getting his Word to us. We just need to be willing to apply it and reprogram our minds.

When I first started renewing my mind, I had to put Post-it notes of handwritten Scriptures on my mirror that I needed to keep foremost in my mind. I kept a list of verses—passages that reminded me who I am in Christ and what I have in Christ. Post-it notes are still my best friend to this very day—because it took years to develop all the wrong thoughts. Despite our best efforts, we can't undo overnight what took so much time to create—all those occurrences of listening to family, friends, teachers, the media, ourselves—so many voices feeding us shame-inducing thoughts. But as I committed to the process of replacing my thoughts with God's thoughts, it has changed the course of my life.

Talk Back

When the lies come, the ones you've believed about yourself—fat, ugly, stupid, worthless, fundamentally flawed, failure, dumb, incapable, inadequate—take those thoughts captive. When someone is taken captive, he or she is still alive but held in confinement, contained and under control. Sometimes our thoughts will not die, but we can control them and take them captive. We have the power to intentionally quit thinking them and think new thoughts based on God's truth. To talk back.

So, talk to yourself. Encourage yourself. Build yourself up. Tell yourself the opposite of all the lies you're hearing . . . "I'm smart. I can do this. I'm strong."

When the past screams . . .

You are hopeless.

You are useless.

You're not good enough.

You'll never measure up.

Tell yourself the truth . . .

- I am alive with Christ. (Ephesians 2:5)
- I am a new creature in Christ. (2 Corinthians 5:17)
- I am the righteousness of God in Christ Jesus.
  (2 Corinthians 5:21)
- Greater is he who is in me than he who is in the world.
  (1 John 4:4)
- It is not I who live, but Christ lives in me.
  (Galatians 2:20)
- I am greatly loved by God. (Romans 1:7; Ephesians 2:4;
  Colossians 3:12)
- I can do all things through Christ Jesus.
  (Philippians 4:13)
- I am God's workmanship, created in Christ for good
  works. (Ephesians 2:10)
- I am more than a conqueror through him who loves
  me. (Romans 8:37)

Just last week, I wrote out eighty-five of God's promises to carry with me in my notebook. Why, after all these years, is that still so important to me? Because when the devil is screaming his accusations every second, it's important to counteract them with God's voice.

As I said earlier, when God moves in, we move on. It really is possible to learn to think a new way. But you're going to have to start thinking about what you are thinking about. Ensure that you board the right train of thought at the start of every day. Make conscious choices and put forth effort to reprogram your mind. Talk to yourself.

"Just because this train filled with doubt, fear, insecurity, bitterness, offense, discouragement, negativity, and anger pulled into the platform of my mind doesn't mean I'm getting on it. In fact, I'm *not* getting on it. The enemy has taken me on that train many times in years past, so I know where it ends up—and today I'm just not getting on that train."

Instead, think: *"Whatever is true, whatever is noble, whatever is right, whatever is pure, whatever is lovely, whatever is admirable—if anything is excellent or praiseworthy—think about such things"* (Philippians 4:8).

I get up every day and pick the train I really want to take. I talk to myself the truth that I know, the truth that sets me free—and I jump tracks as many times a day as necessary to stay on course. Make up your mind today to set your course every morning, because there's nothing more powerful than a made-up mind.

My Daddy Says . . .

Because we know how fiercely the enemy fights for our minds, Nick and I have taught our girls, Catherine and Sophia, the power of God's truth since they were babies. Every day, we tell our daughters who they are based on God's Word—who they are in Christ—using verses among the list

I gave you. We build them up and affirm them as beautiful, strong young women in God.

Not only do we teach them verses *from* God's Word about who they are, but we intentionally have spoken truth to them *based on* God's Word about their worth and value.

Nick is a great dad, and there is not a single day that he does not tell Catherine and Sophia how much he loves them, how beautiful, bold, courageous, intelligent, and awesome they are. He is a totally biased dad, and I love him for that. He has fun with our girls. He enjoys them and that reassures them, building their confidence and feelings of being loved. Each time I watch him interact with our girls, I catch a glimpse of the Father heart of God toward us.

I remember once, when our daughter Catherine was in kindergarten, a boy in her class grabbed a toy away from her and said, "You're just dumb and ugly."

As a mother, as a woman who had battled shame most of my life, you can imagine how I felt when I heard this. My course was set in kindergarten—and it was not a good course. The lessons I learned in kindergarten: all those shame-filled emotions connected to being singled out, rejected, and judged; the images of me holding my feta sandwich, feeling so uncovered, vulnerable, sitting under the stares of all my classmates. Oh the pain at hearing she was bullied. I remembered how at that same age and stage in life, I had jumped on the wrong train of thought and stayed on it for years and years.

But not Catherine. She stayed on the course that had

been set. She didn't take on any shame. She stood up to that boy.

"No, I'm not," she answered. "My daddy says I'm beautiful and intelligent."

She may have been only five years old, but she was old enough to know and understand and believe what her daddy told her every single day. She knew the truth in her heart, and she was confident and bold to speak it. She didn't get on the same shame train I did in kindergarten, and consequently, that single moment of refuting the lie with the truth has potentially saved my daughter years of trying to prove to every guy that she really is neither dumb nor ugly. Who knows where that train of thought would have taken her if she had jumped on board.

I wonder how different my own school experience would have been if I had known to do that very same thing. Although I cannot change my past experiences or responses, I am so grateful to God that I did finally choose to get off the shame train of thoughts and embark on the process of renewing my mind. I am so grateful that I have committed myself to the hard work of 2 Corinthians 10:5: *"We demolish arguments and every pretension that sets itself up against the knowledge of God, and we take captive every thought to make it obedient to Christ."*

If I hadn't started that journey, then I am sure Catherine's response would have been different that day. It has not been an easy journey. Learning to take rogue thoughts captive and making them obedient to Christ rarely is. I have had to be as disciplined, vigilant, and focused as any law enforcement officer chasing a fugitive. When I heard about Catherine's response that day, I knew that it was worth all the effort I had exerted. I had made a choice to choose life and now my children were flourishing just as God promised me in Deuteronomy 30:19. While my old default mechanism would have been to believe the lie at her age, she refuted it. She knows she is a beloved daughter—and I do too.

Through strengthening my heart and soul, and renewing my mind, God has taught me that though I cannot change the past, I don't have to perpetuate it into my future. I can change my mind, my future, and the next generation's heritage. I can love the Lord my God with all my heart, soul, and mind. I can grow strong for the challenges that lie ahead in my promised land. Yes, I know, just as the children of Israel discovered, that to defeat my enemy of shame there will always be walls to tear down and giants to slay. But I'll be ready. Like Catherine, I know what my Daddy says.

Chapter 9

TEAR DOWN
THE WALLS

I love to run—with friends, alone, on a trail, anytime, anywhere. I love the challenge and the press of reaching new milestones and levels of exertion, so I know what it's like to hit a wall. It's that roadblock moment mid-run that's actually a form of collapse of the entire system: body and form, brains and emotion. Your legs feel like concrete, your breathing becomes labored, and you begin to shuffle. It's where the brain works fine, but the legs up and quit.

When you hit a wall, you have two choices: keep going even though you feel your strides shift into small steps, or give in to all the negative thoughts flooding your mind and stop. Your body is responding to the press—and it's telling you it needs the energy to overcome.

So often in our spiritual lives, we experience the same thing. We get saved and start a good run—out of Egypt and right through the wilderness, building our heart, soul, and mind muscles as we go. We build up our stamina, character, and fruit of the Spirit output. We start to advance, grow, and mature in our spiritual journey. Things really seem to be flourishing in many areas of our lives.

Then we hit a wall.

That internal roadblock moment where everything seems like it should still keep moving forward, but it won't . . . because we are holding back something somewhere. We progress forward in some areas, but maybe not in one particular part of our life—and in reality, that one area is impacting all the others.

I know this pattern; it's a constant rhythm of growth in our lives. Indeed, I've experienced walls many times in my life, and I've come to realize that they consistently lead to greater maturity and freedom. God always has something greater on the other side of a wall. But the year Nick and I were preparing to be married, I hit a wall bigger than any I'd ever encountered before—the one that could have stopped me from stepping into my purpose.

No one was more surprised than I was. I was being promoted to director of a statewide youth movement, and I really thought that all the spiritual hard work was behind me. God had done such a powerful healing in my life, and his presence was so real to me. My focus had shifted dramatically from the pain of my past to my hopes for the future. Gifts of leadership and teaching were developing at a rapid pace. My days weren't problem-free, of course, but with each new challenge I could see the positive change in me.

And that's when I hit the wall.

I never saw it. I never expected to hit a wall of any kind, but sometimes when God is ready to move us into another area of our promised land, this is exactly what happens. Territory is needed for the next phase of our journey, and the wall between us and that additional land has to come down.

I know that God uses his perfect timing—not ours—to heal our broken hearts, wounded souls, and tormented minds—and I had come a long way in those areas. But I couldn't keep going. There was some kind of invisible, inner, towering wall in my way—and I kept hitting it.

No matter how hard I tried to move forward, I didn't have whatever I needed to overcome. I was stuck.

Though I was delivered, I was not free. Like the children of Israel, I had left Egypt and captivity, made it through the wilderness, but I was not living in all the freedom Jesus had purchased for me. I had entered the edge of my promised land—where the city of Jericho was with its towering walls—but I hadn't yet truly possessed the promise.

Yet, I was determined to move forward into my promised land.

I had to figure out how.

I had to identify the wall.

The Wall of Unforgiveness

UNFORGIVENESS. I'm not talking about *unforgiveness* in lower case letters—forgiving an unkind word or a thoughtless foible of a friend or coworker, or even someone's intentional effort to wrong me. I had learned the importance of forgiveness, and I had been growing in my ability to express it. No, my wall was UNFORGIVENESS—the all-caps variety—that seemed beyond my reach to change. Its roots dug far back into my childhood and ran deep into the formation of my soul.

I realized that even though I was delivered—I was no longer being abused—I was still carrying the shame of the abuse into each new day, because I was harboring unforgiveness toward my abusers. And while I held on to unforgiveness, the abusers were still mentally holding on to me. To be truly liberated, I needed to let go and forgive. But I didn't really know how.

When I became a follower of Jesus, I wanted to fight that unforgiveness. I tried to fight it. But I failed time and again. Oh, I could forgive petty offenses, minor infractions, and daily things that happen here and there. But this felt completely different. I could not forgive the perpetrators of the abuse that happened to me—and I felt deeply ashamed because of it. I knew that as a Christian I was supposed to forgive, but I could not.

Entering into new territory in my promised land—preparing for marriage and being promoted to director—made it hard to ignore anymore. Yes, I was flourishing in ministry, but now my personal life was about to be intimately shared with another person, and God knew I needed to deal with some unresolved residue. I was unknowingly reacting to Nick from that place of unforgiveness toward my abusers. I didn't want him to control me or really direct me because of the residue of abuse. But if that wall didn't come down, and I didn't forgive, then I would be punishing Nick by my behavior for something he never did. My reactions, responses, and understanding were rooted in unforgiveness—and he didn't deserve that. I had never been close enough to anyone for all of this to be exposed.

God knew I had to deal with the toxins in my heart if I was to move forward, but I didn't want to open that wound. I didn't want to go inward and deal with that wall.

When I got saved, I denied I had unforgiveness. I filed the matter in the "it's under the blood" category (1 John 1:7). I put it in the file of "forgetting things that are behind" (Philippians 3:13). Those verses and concepts are true in the right context, but I wasn't free, and I was using them to avoid dealing with my unforgiveness. I wanted to pretend I had dealt with it; however, avoiding something is really just denial—and that never gets us anywhere in the promised land.

That wall of unforgiveness towered over me, and God knew I needed to circle back and deal with it to move forward. I wasn't sure I could face it. But his promise remained sure whether I obeyed or not: *"If we confess our sins, he is faithful and just and will forgive us our sins and purify us from all unrighteousness"* (1 John 1:9).

I kept seeking God. I prayed. I searched his Word.

Unforgiveness continued to block my way to my promised land.

It was all I could see.

How could I possibly forgive my abusers?

And, even worse, I realized that this question had its roots in a more treacherous question: How could I forgive *God* for letting the abuse happen?

That question so frightened me that I dared not say it aloud to myself or anyone else. But there it stood. I could not face it because I feared that it would take me to a place that would ruin me: *If God had allowed such a horrible thing to happen to me, then God must have a dark side. How could he really be good? How could he really be trustworthy?*

I knew the Word, but knowing it wasn't helping me. God had forgiven me, and I knew I should be able to forgive others. *"But if you do not forgive others their sins, your Father will not forgive your sins"* (Matthew 6:15). Still I felt justified in my unforgiveness.

It was just so hard.

So there I stood, facing my wall: wanting the freedom God had promised, wanting the greater opportunities that waited beyond the wall, but unable to do what was necessary for God to take it down.

Delivered But Not Yet Free

I was just like the children of Israel when they wanted to enter the Promised Land. They were no longer in captivity but weren't yet home. They were delivered from slavery but not yet living in the fullness of the freedom that was theirs. It was better than where they had been but not as good as it was going to be.

I too was delivered in this area . . . but not yet free.

The Israelites had made great progress getting across the Jordan River, experiencing a miracle when God blocked the water miles upriver to allow them to cross on dry ground (Joshua 4). They had paused on the plains of Jericho and obeyed more instructions from God to prepare to take the land—including circumcising all males, celebrating a Passover meal, and saying farewell to manna (Joshua 5).

Finally, the Promised Land seemed to be within reach.

And then they hit a wall—just like I did.

When the soldiers got their first view of the city, it was buttoned up tight: *"Now the gates of Jericho were securely barred because of the Israelites. No one went out and no one came in"* (Joshua 6:1).

The walls were a very real impenetrable force surrounding the entire city of Jericho. They were made of heavy mud bricks designed to keep any enemy out. Though the height varied, some believe it may have been thirty feet at its highest, and the thickness was about five feet. What's more, a deep perimeter trench circled the wall. Think moat with no water.[1]

Jericho had heard the Israelites were coming, so the place was on lockdown. The Israelites could see that the scenario they faced was impossible. Swords against a mighty wall—no contest.

Isn't this just like God?

Yet, God had promised them the land—freedom—just as he promised freedom for you and me.

So just when the people thought, *At last! After forty years in the wilderness, we're about to make our first conquest. This is awesome!* God said, "I want you to take that new territory right over there, right behind that massive, impenetrable, unscalable wall."

It's not as if the circumstances were in doubt—that wall was a real deal-breaker. Too high to climb over, too thick to dig through—the situation was impossible. They no doubt felt as I did when told I needed to forgive my abusers: "But Lord, how can I do what I cannot do?"

The same way God wants us to do everything—not by our might but by his Spirit (Zechariah 4:6). His power is made perfect in our weakness (2 Corinthians 13:4). It is when faced with the impossible that we experience the power of the Holy Spirit firsthand—when we face walls that we have no hope of tearing down on our own.

When God began readying the Israelites for battle, he said to Joshua, *"See, I have delivered Jericho into your hands, along with its king and its fighting men"* (Joshua 6:2).

That verse always makes me laugh. I picture the Israelites looking at each other with puzzled expressions. "See? See *what?* All I see is a wall!"

But God wanted them to see not with their eyes but with their faith. He wanted them to see that even though the circumstances were impossible, he would give them the promised victory, because all things are possible to him who believes (Mark 9:23).

If there's one key to watching the walls in your life fall, to moving forward in freedom, to seeing the promises of God at work, then this is it: *You must learn to believe the truth of God's Word over the facts of your circumstances.* You have to look to God, not at everything around you. Only then can you see what's going on from his perspective. We have to see that wall torn down even before it is. We have to believe that God is faithful to do what he has promised (Hebrews 10:23).

I had to see myself forgiving my abusers—so that God could take down the wall. I had to see myself free, and on the other side of this great obstacle—just as the children of Israel did.

Do What God Says

As the Israelites began preparing for their battle at Jericho, God began telling them what to see—victory.

Then he told them what to do—*exactly* what to do. I want you to notice that these weren't suggestions for them to consider or a smorgasbord of options for them to choose from. These were specific, definitive instructions.

> *March around the city once with all the armed men. Do this for six days. Have seven priests carry trumpets of rams' horns in front of the ark. On the seventh day, march around the city seven times, with the priests blowing the trumpets. When you hear them sound a long blast on the trumpets, have the whole army give a loud shout; then the wall of the city will collapse and the army will go up, everyone straight in.*
>
> Joshua 6:3–5

Once they'd heard and understood God's instructions, Joshua shouted, *"Advance!"*

And they did. They marched in one big circle all around that wall, lined up as commanded with the armed guard first, the trumpet-blowing priests next, followed by the ark of the covenant, and then the rear guard.

I can't imagine what they were thinking or feeling. I could spend a few pages speculating, but here's the point—it didn't matter! It didn't matter if it made sense to them or not, if they understood *how* this would work, if they thought it was a wise plan or a foolish one, if they thought it made them look courageous or like idiots. The only thing that mattered is that *they did what God said*. They willingly obeyed.

> *So he had the ark of the LORD carried around the city, circling it once. Then the army returned to camp and spent the night there.*
>
> Joshua 6:11

And they did the same thing on day two.

And repeated it on day three.

And on days four and five and six.

And on the seventh day, as God had instructed, they circled the wall seven times instead of one.

> *The seventh time around, when the priests sounded the trumpet blast, Joshua commanded the army, "Shout! For the LORD has given you the city!" . . .*
>
> *When the trumpets sounded, the army shouted, and at the sound of the trumpet, when the men gave a loud*

shout, the wall collapsed; so everyone charged straight in, and they took the city.

Joshua 6:16, 20

And the wall, as the old church song goes, came tumbling down! The wall was nothing but rubble.

And the Israelite soldiers *charged* straight in.

That's how God handled *their* wall.

So what about your wall? How do you take it down?

By doing exactly what God says.

Search God's Word for instructions and just do it. Whether it makes sense to you or not, whether you understand *how* it works or *why* it works, whether you think it's a wise plan or a foolish one, whether it makes you look courageous or like an idiot. No matter what vulnerability it requires. The only thing that matters is that you *do what God says*. That you willingly obey. That's what I did—and it required that I trust him in a way I never had.

The Cycle of Growth

Learning to truly trust God has been one of my greatest challenges on my way to shame-free living and freedom. When you've lived in the prison of shame for as long as I had, you've developed many broken defense mechanisms—such as never being truly vulnerable to anyone, or controlling everything you can in your life so that you will not be hurt again. These mechanisms provide a false set of comfort that you cannot fathom letting go of for an unknown future. You cannot imagine that there is security and safety "out there" in which you can actually rest. And you cannot possess the promises of a God you do not trust.

Learning to trust takes experience. Lots of experience.

Learning to trust takes repetition.

Learning to trust takes failing.

Learning to trust takes challenges, trials, and tests.

Learning to trust takes risking—following God in the face of our fear.

Learning to trust takes time—lots and lots of it.

Trust has to grow. And in my observation—and personal experience—for those who've struggled with shame, trust grows slowly.

But here's the great news. *God knows how to grow trust.* He knows how to plant it, how to nourish it, how to repair it when it's been broken, and how to restore it when it's been lost. God is in the trust-growing business!

Do you know what he uses to grow our trust? He uses the very tool that the enemy uses to try to stop us. He uses our fear. Fear exposes the limits of our present capacity—but not our potential capacity.

Think about this: When you come face to face with fear, do you know what you are looking at? You are looking at the very next place where God is preparing to build your trust.

He's been building mine for years.

Trust-building is a process. A journey. For all of us.

If we are not prepared to go through the metamorphosis required to walk in freedom, we will soon long for the familiar routines of our former prisons. We won't trust, and we will return to our shame again and again.

So what must we do?

*We must put more faith in what we **do** know about God than in what we **don't** know about the future.* We must walk in obedience, trusting that God is good and there is no darkness in him at all (1 John 1:5). God doesn't have a dark side. He can only do good, and only good will come of the things he asks us to do.

Trust is what the children of Israel had to do to walk laps around Jericho. Trust is what I was going to have to do to forgive and be free. Pressing through our fear each time and cycling through this pattern of choosing to obey so we can grow is how we continue to mature. The longer we walk with God, the stronger our trust grows, and the smaller our fear shrinks. Our faith develops. We're not moved by what struck fear in our hearts years ago, but there remains land ahead of us that God wants us to possess, so there will inevitably be different fears we will need to overcome. There will always be new areas where we will need to trust God.

I've had to trust God to overcome my past, to open doors of opportunity for ministry, to bring me the right husband, to help me be a wife, to parent my babies. Now, I have to trust him to give me wisdom to parent a teenager, to run a global anti-trafficking organization, to lead me with Propel Women. This is the life in Christ we signed up for . . . fear, trust, repeat. It's a cycle of growth—a faith adventure—we go through over and over again in our lifetime.

When it came to forgiving my abusers, I needed faith to

obey and forgive. There was only one way for God to tear down my wall. I had to act like the children of Israel did and do what God said to do. I had to trust him.

I Fought to Forgive

As I pursued the ability to forgive my abusers, the enemy was persistent, convincing, sneaky, and treacherous. He was fighting to keep the territory he'd owned for a very long time, and he fought dirty and hard. I had to get to a place where the memory of my abusers could no longer trigger shame and shame-producing behaviors in me and hold me back spiritually, emotionally, and relationally.

A war raged in my mind where all the shame-filled thoughts screamed . . .

- Hopelessness: *You'll never get over this, you know. You've tried for years. You are reaching for the impossible. If you were going to be able to forgive, you would have done it by now. You've been stuck too long.*

- Blame: *You'll always hold this against them because you should! They got away with it. They deserve to be hated. They aren't worthy of your forgiveness. This just lets them off the hook.*

- Victimization: *Of course you can't forgive them. How could you after all they did to you? Because of them, you are broken, damaged, and weak. You can't be expected to forgive. You are far too wounded.*

- Doubt: *This kind of forgiveness doesn't really happen. It's just some religious ideal cooked up by spiritual leaders to make you keep coming back for more. People who claim to have forgiven their abusers are either living in denial or lying to seem more spiritual than they really are.*

- Justification: *Give it up and just accept that it's okay to resent and hate. Bitterness and rage are simply the natural human responses to being wronged—and you were so wronged.*

- Self-recrimination: *You brought the abuse on yourself, you know. It only happened because you let it happen, because you are weak, because you didn't stop it, didn't avoid it, let them get away with it. You forgive them? Don't even go there. You're not even qualified to forgive, because you are as much to blame as they are.*

My point is this: When you are readying yourself to possess God's promise of shame-free living, the enemy will pull every trick in the book to *distract* you from following through. Why? Because he knows he cannot *defeat* you—because Jesus has already defeated him.

But you have to press through in obedience to his Word. I had to forgive.

I did everything I knew how to do. Just as the children of Israel circled Jericho, I kept marching forward. I continued to search the Scripture for answers and help. I listened to countless sermons about forgiveness. I read books on forgiveness by Christians whose faith I respected. I prayed and prayed and prayed, my prayers grounded in the promises of God's Word.

Forgiveness, I've learned, is not for the faint of heart. Our legs have to keep running to carry us there. Taking responsibility to forgive those who've wronged us is, to put it bluntly, a lot of very hard work. But I wasn't on my own. Sometimes we need help to tear down our walls!

God led me to a counselor, a woman known for her deeply spiritual, prayer-based ministry to those who had suffered trauma. It was another lap. One day, as she and I were in deep prayer together, I experienced a vivid memory of one specific, horrific event of abuse. I started sobbing, describing the scene to her, reliving the emotions of the little girl I had been.

"God does not care. He does not care!" I said, my body heaving with sobs. "I cried out to God in that room, asking him to stop this from happening to me. But it didn't stop."

"Where is Jesus in this scene?" the counselor asked.

All of a sudden, in my mind's eye, while seeing every detail of the room where the abuse was occurring, I saw Jesus there too. In the room. Jesus too was weeping. He was weeping for me. He was weeping for all the pain and all the wrong that sin was doing to me—to this little girl he loved.

Something broke inside of me; something hard and rigid melted at that moment. Jesus *saw* me in that room. He cared deeply, and it broke his heart. He agonized with me. The abuse happened not because I was bad or because he did not care. Bad things happen in a sin-bent, fallen world, and those bad things grieve him deeply. It mattered to him. *I* mattered to him. He had never let me out of his sight—ever. I saw it for myself, and it changed me in this deeply affected area forever. He had been guiding me to this moment of freedom all of my life. He loved me that much!

The writer of Hebrews tells us to look to God, *"fixing our eyes on Jesus, the pioneer and perfecter of faith. For the joy set before him he endured the cross, **scorning its shame**, and sat down at the right hand of the throne of God"* (Hebrews 12:2, emphasis added).

I love it! *Jesus shamed shame!* He declared shame, not us, as fundamentally flawed! He scorned it. How beautiful! No wonder the enemy's heart shudders with fear when we start really getting free. Not only does he lose his power to shame us, but Jesus turns it back on him.

I cannot adequately explain my encounter seeing Jesus in the room with my abuser. It goes beyond words. I can only tell you that at that moment, God did what only God can do. God did *a supernatural thing* in me. God infused me with his light and increased my faith in his goodness. Suddenly I knew in my heart, soul, and mind that there is no dark side to God; he had not turned his back and looked the other way. What had happened to me *was* dark, but when Jesus looked upon the scene of my abuse, his light was shining—his light of compassion, his light of breaking free of the darkness of the grave so that he could forever shatter the darkness of sin. He knew that one day I too would live fully in his light, where no darkness could ever touch me again. And he knew something even more mysterious—that he would turn around what the enemy meant for evil and destruction, and use it so that his brilliant light would shine out through every one of my broken places!

I saw that day that what the apostle John said is true: *"This is the message we have heard from him and declare to you: God is light; in him there is no darkness at all"* (1 John 1:5). The fact that God is light, without *any* darkness at all, meant that he had nothing to hide from me. He could not hurt me. He would not hurt me. Unlike my abusers, he did not have a dark side. I could trust him totally. His light would enable me to walk through dark places. No more covering up, hiding, shirking reality. I would face whatever God uncovered, no matter how painful, because what he reveals is for my good.

Now, my friend, I want you to see the victory of this moment. But I also want you to see the *reality* of this moment—the reality of this warfare we are called to fight this side of heaven. You need to know that I did not walk out of the counselor's office that day with forgiveness for my abusers pouring out of me. Not yet! *But I was closer to that freedom!* And I kept going. It was another lap.

Fighting for our personal freedom from shame is a choice that we make, and we make it over and over and over again. *And that's all right!* This is expected from here until heaven, *and there is no shame in this process—in this journey!*

We all have walls to overcome—those seemingly impenetrable forces standing between us and our freedom from shame. They can be walls of sin, as my unforgiveness was, or a circumstance in our lives we have to emotionally and physically overcome—such as being a single mom, or suffering a great financial loss, or losing a job. Walls are anything that have the power to make us feel trapped in shame. They can be rooted in something we did or in something done to us. Either way, their sheer height and thickness make them ominous to us until that turning-point moment when we trust God like never before in that area—when we believe the power of his Word more than we believe in the power of our circumstances.

As long as I held on to my unforgiveness, I was carrying my abusers and their impact on my life into each and every day. Subsequently, I was empowering the enemy to overcome me with shame-filled feelings. But when I forgave, I was no longer giving the enemy a foothold. The wall of unforgiveness came down, and I was now free from shame in that area of my life.

I know so many courageous women who have faced a wall—and watched it come down—all because they chose to pursue God and obey what he told them to do. It was never easy, but they chose to put more faith in what they knew about God—about his trustworthy nature—than in what they didn't know about their future. They bravely chose to run to God—not away from him—even when everything inside wanted to hunker down and self-protect. They chose to allow him to soften their hearts—even in the midst of immense pain. They allowed him to define who they were rather than their circumstances or failures.

My friend Heather is one of those women. She is an amazing wife with a beautiful family, working alongside her husband as together they serve in ministry. She is a flourishing leader who ministers to women in a powerful way. But the day she hit a wall was the beginning of becoming who she is today. Had she not faced her wall more than a decade ago, she would have never fulfilled her passion, purpose, and potential.

Just a year after her wedding, Heather found herself locked in a psych ward with nothing but herself—no husband, no purse, no wallet, no iPhone. Curled in a fetal position, clad only in a hospital gown, absolutely alone. The ambulance had dropped her off like a delivery package.

Nut house.

Looney bin.

The labels haunted her.

The shame engulfed her.

That moment was the culmination of a lifelong struggle. She had begun to have her first suicidal thoughts at age eight. Her first suicide attempt was at age fourteen, her next at age twenty-three.

She had lived with the stigma of mental illness since childhood. The shame had always been suffocating, driving her into isolation and compounding her self-destructing temptations. But that day in a cold, lonely room, as she faced white concrete walls that stood as towering reminders of the wall of mental illness, a new desire arose within her to acknowledge that she needed help—spiritually, mentally, and medically. She began to find the courage to confront the stigma that imprisoned her in shame and receive the help she needed. Desperate, she cried out to God—the only one who could truly set her free.

Heather left that hospital and stepped into the care of

health professionals and spiritual leaders—as well as the unconditional love of her husband. With their help, she faithfully combined daily prayer, daily medication, weekly journaling, weekly church, and monthly Christian counseling to overcome and maintain her freedom. She continues all of these strategies to this day, because she never wants to face that particular wall again. She writes a successful blog that addresses and raises awareness about mental illness— and ministers spiritual comfort and healing to women who face the wall she watched God bring down. Powerful. Making a difference. Lifting shame off women fighting a stigma she personally understands.

Heather's wall wasn't sin, as was mine, but like any wall, it debilitated her growth. It was something that made her feel trapped in shame; something she had to face in order for God to be able to tear it down. She obeyed that stirring in her heart to risk and reach out for help—just like I did. It was the beginning of her journey to freedom.

My friend Natalie faced a completely different wall. Having grown up in the south, where being married and having children was the expected culmination of virtue and success for every young woman, Natalie's passions took her on a career path that skipped marriage and children and landed her as an attorney and deputy chief of staff to a sitting US governor.

She had dreamed of being a lawyer since she was a child— often sneaking out of bed to watch *Matlock* and *Law and Order*. Of course, her immediate family was extremely proud of all her success, but for years at every large group gathering, people asked when she would marry, because, well, that was the most important goal for every "good southern girl." Most never asked about her professional accomplishments or lofty ambitions. She hated how those "marriage" questions, and the whispers behind her back, made her feel like something was terribly wrong with her. As if singleness were somehow a disease and she was to be pitied.

The wall that the stigma of singleness built over time was daunting to Natalie. She didn't know how to get around it, climb over it, or get away from it. By the time she was a bridesmaid in her seventeenth wedding, she began to wonder if all those people were right—that there was something wrong with her. As she watched her two younger brothers marry, the shame only grew.

As she turned thirty, and found herself the single girl among all her married friends, she entered a very dark and lonely period. She questioned all the decisions she'd made— ones she'd thought God had led her to make. She questioned if she'd somehow missed God's will and purpose for her life. She put every facet of her life on trial—including God.

She had hit a wall.

After much soul-searching, prayer, and reflection, Natalie came to understand that her completion is in Christ alone and not another person, including a husband (Philippians 1:6). That this season of singleness is a gift and not a source of shame. That society, tradition, and cultural expectations do not define you, but who you are in Christ defines you. As she faced the wall of singleness and all the feelings of shame it represented—and exchanged all the lies of shame for the truth of God's unconditional acceptance and affirmation—God brought the wall tumbling down.

Natalie is still single, and encourages other single professionals in the importance of knowing who they are in Christ. She continues to flourish professionally, and who knows if her future will be in the Oval Office one day—whether single or married.

Do you see how vastly different our walls can be? They are as different as our life experiences—and the twisted lies the enemy tells us about our worth and value in light of our circumstances. The enemy will use anything to build a wall in our lives—infertility, an eating disorder, anxiety, depression, addiction, poverty. He will always tell you that your wall is the one that cannot come down. But that's not true. Any wall, no matter how impossible it seems, can come down—whether it's related to your self-image, an abortion you had, a divorce you never expected, or an affair you regret.

Maybe a memory or present circumstance in your life condemns you daily, telling you it has a right to remain because you didn't pray enough or fast enough. Just another lie. Just another wall.

The enemy's tactics are relentless, but he's no match for the power of Jesus Christ alive in our lives. We have to trust, obey, and put more faith in our God who can tear down our wall than in the power of the wall to keep us imprisoned. We have to fight for our personal freedom from shame. That's exactly what I did. And what Heather did. And what Natalie did.

So, what's your story? What's your wall? Does it look too big?

Your God is bigger than your wall.

Does it look impossible?

Impossible is where God starts.

Do you need a miracle?

Good. Because miracles are what God does.

Remember, it's not by might, nor by power, but by his Spirit that you overcome shame. Trust and obey him, and your wall will come tumbling down!

Chapter 10

THE BUNGEE CORD OF SHAME

The instructor tightened my harness. Excitement had raced through me all the way up the climb to the top of the Auckland Bridge. I had thought of bungee jumping for some time, and speaking at a youth camp in Auckland, New Zealand, allowed for the perfect opportunity. I mentioned it to the kids as I was teaching that week and they egged me on.

The only problem was I don't like things that come flying back at me when I least expect it.

As we climbed a special designed walkway under the bridge, the view of the Waitemata Harbour was spectacular. It looked so much bigger from this vantage point—versus driving across the bridge in a car or looking across from the shore. It was almost more than my eyes could take in.

The excitement and adrenalin was building in me. I couldn't stop looking in every direction. I felt so powerful, so courageous—as if I were about to do something no one else had ever done! Even though they had.

At the end of the walkway, we entered a steel room built under the bridge, with a retractable platform called the jumping pod. It had been built specifically for jumping underneath the bridge, as all the while traffic passed overhead.

There the instructor explained release papers and provided a table for us to sign them. I barely comprehended anything. I kept looking at the amazing views . . . and the guy they just let go off the gangplank, or was that a diving board?

This wasn't as I had imagined it at all.

As I stared at the signature line on the papers, I wondered, *Were they for signing my life away? Or for someone to call if I didn't make it?* I wasn't entirely sure, but if you didn't sign, you didn't jump! So sign I did.

Was I actually going to walk the plank?

I watched as the guy who had just jumped went under water half the length of his body.

You bungeed into the water!

I didn't remember reading about that part.

And then, he was flying back toward all of us who were watching.

I was starting to feel unsure . . .

The thing about a bungee cord is when it does come back at you, it's like a surprise attack. You try to be prepared for it, but you're never quite able to predict its timing, its elasticity, its speed—just like shame.

When Shame Surprises You

I don't like surprises—of any kind. I know it's a residual symptom of abuse, but I have a hard time relaxing and enjoying something that surprises me, even when it's a good one like a surprise birthday party.

And when it's shame, I definitely don't like it. Especially when it comes out of nowhere—like some crazy bridge-jumping bungee cord. You walk through a certain degree of freedom, throw off shame, and it comes flying back at you when you least expect it, when you never saw it coming. (Which is part of why I chickened out that day on the bridge and didn't jump!)

But even though we don't like these surprise attacks, we can learn to face them and not let shame take us out. I'm sure when the children of Israel got to the Promised Land and saw the walls and giants, they were surprised. They had made it through the wilderness, which they thought was a terrible place, but there were no giants in the wilderness.

Now they were up against the descendants of Anak, people of great physical size (Genesis 6:4; Numbers 13:33), known to be bullies and tyrants who specialized in intimidation and cruelty. Part of seven people groups who lived in the land—the Canaanites, Hittites, Hivites, Perizzites, Girgashites, Amorites, and Jebusites—they represent all of the giants we face throughout our lives, each designed to make us feel shame even though Jesus took it from us.

Personally, I've encountered many giants through the

years—rejection, fear, feeling less than, not good enough—and they all produce feelings of shame, even though I've long been free and in my promised land.

The promised land represents that place in our spiritual journey—in every area of our lives—where we are now mature enough to live a victorious Christian life. Yes, we are free from shame; we've dropped our baggage in the wilderness and picked up our freedom. But the enemy will never stop trying to make us *experience* shame—and fear—by using giants to make us try to run and hide. His tactics haven't changed since the garden of Eden when Adam and Eve felt naked and afraid, and then hid from God.

Shame and fear. Always together. Always the enemy's weapons of choice.

Yet even if we slay every giant we identify, there will always be new ones. Even if we slay the giant of rejection who makes us feel not good enough in one situation, then a new giant will step up to harass us in another. The next giant will have a new name—but always a name that produces debilitating shame. There always will be bullies who try to intimidate us, who make us feel small and less than. And they will come again and again like a bungee cord—smacking us in the head, flying out of nowhere, when we least expect it.

Sometimes shame can be out of sight and out of mind for days, weeks, or even years—only to sneak up from behind, knocking us off our feet. You know what I'm talking about. You can be walking in a healthy level of self-esteem (freedom), but then you're passed up for a promotion, fail in a new endeavor, encounter someone who calls you out on social media, read a negative review, let someone down, or disappoint a loved one. Immediately, the bungee cord of shame comes flying back at you and your thoughts flood with, *Not good enough, never will be; you just don't have it; go ahead and give up.*

I used to recoil at the reappearance of old shame, but over the past twenty-five years of my ongoing journey of becoming shame-free, I've experienced a "knowing" entwined with that pain—so much so that I have come to understand there's a purpose when that bungee cord brings old shame flying back. I've learned to anticipate the healing God is about to do in me—if I let him.

Every time I come face to face with a new shame trigger situation, such as when:

- Someone I trust unexpectedly rejects me;
- I am misunderstood, overlooked, or criticized;
- I don't live up to someone's expectations;
- I'm struggling to complete a manuscript;
- I talk and begin to feel like a failure.

I'm willing to consider and discover what God is up to. Even when it hurts, when it's painful, when I am afraid, when I cry, when I tremble in the face of conflict, when I see the worst in others or in myself. I know God is up to something, further conforming me to his image—to the image he originally created me to be before all this shame filling ever started.

How like God, then, to make sure that while I was writing a book on this subject, I not only was living the principles that I am teaching you, but also I was challenged to apply them to myself in a struggle. Have I mentioned that, although I am free, I am still walking out that freedom? That I am not so healed I don't need Jesus every single moment of every single day?

We live in a pain-filled, fallen world—and sometimes we experience that up close and personal—but God's Word is true no matter our circumstances. I've experienced the power of his Word and the confidence of his truths through recovery from sexual abuse, miscarriage, grief, spiritual and emotional abuse, danger, troubled relationships, conflict, betrayal, disappointment, and loss. No matter how great the trial, I'm convinced *that the testing of my faith produces perseverance and that I must let perseverance finish its work so that I may be mature and complete, not lacking anything* (James 1:2–4).

Because I'm willing to work through new shame triggers, new insights take hold. New strengths take root. Each step forward I take with God, I discover that his love is deeper than I knew, that his forgiveness is more complete than I'd dared to hope, that his grace is richer than I'd ever imagined.

Today, I am one day closer to *not lacking anything.*

As I continued to work on this book, God revealed that

some of those wounds from shame in my past simply had a Band-Aid over them. They were not yet healed. I had learned to live so well with the pain from some of my shame-wounds that I didn't realize I was limping . . . until I got around some people who were running.

During the writing process, I did a lot of soul searching with God. I spent months talking through things with Nick and I enlisted the help of a counselor. How could I write a book on being healed of shame unless I was willing to stay accountable to the process of healing and practice the very principles I am teaching?

God wanted to make sure that I wasn't asking the victims of trafficking we work with in A21 to undergo a process for healing that I wasn't walking through myself. You cannot take people where you are not prepared to go yourself.

And what about Propel Women? Here we were launching a new initiative to help women internalize a leadership identity and fulfill their purpose, passion, and potential. If I was going to help women who lead deal with their internal issues, then this woman who leads would have to deal with her own.

And on top of all that I was double-checking about my inner self with Nick and a counselor, I was hurt in a relationship I valued. Test time! Smack! That invisible bungee cord brought that old shame out of nowhere and blindsided me, exposing some old wounds I'd thought were long healed. Challenges will do that. They'll apply new pressure to old scars until we discover we aren't completely healed after all.

Residue of old shame, toxic waste that I thought I'd cleaned up and shipped off to Jesus, was revealed—all during the writing of this book!

So much emotion came with this hurt. Especially the emotion of shame—and it was loud just like a shame-producing giant always is.

I was so tempted to interpret that I was being negatively judged. I was sensitive to and fearful of rejection and criticism—and wanted to withdraw. I began to feel I was the problem. I started to slide into my black-and-white perspectives of whether I was either loved or unloved, accepted or rejected, wanted or unwanted—with no rational zone in between these extremes. I began to be tempted to make adjustments to make others feel more comfortable, to people-please. So many of my shame buttons were being pushed all at once!

Shame had shown up once again, camped out on my doorstep, and pounded on the door! And perfectionism, not to be left out of the party, decided to make an appearance as well. Now it was a giant party! (Pun intended.)

Do you know how challenging it is to decide to write a book on shame and then almost not write it, thinking that because you still sometimes struggle with shame yourself, you're not qualified? Imagine that—being too ashamed to write on being free from shame! If shame were easily dealt with, I wouldn't be writing this—I wouldn't need to. But I am—and not because I've found easy answers to wiping shame out of my life. They aren't easy! Rather, I'm writing because I've found God's rich rewards in the ongoing journey from a shame-filled to a shame-free life.

I have found that no matter how big the giant looms over me—no matter how hard he tries to drown out what God wants to say to me—the truth remains: Jesus shamed my shame! So I wrote this book from a place of victory—inside my promised land—to help give you, dear reader, your victory.

I have personally gone through everything I am asking you to do. And I went through it again at an entirely new level as the writing progressed. I purposely chose to go deeper, take more ground in my heart for Jesus and freedom.

And, in the process, I learned even more . . .

Shame-based thinking would declare that bungee-cord shame is terrible news. It would have us sigh in self-disgust, berate ourselves for our weakness, and chastise ourselves for repeating those same old patterns. But shame-free thinking applies a whole new lens to the way we see this situation.

Paul says it well when writing to believers in Philippi:

In all my prayers for all of you, I always pray with joy because of your partnership in the gospel from the first day until now, being confident of this, that he who began a good work in you will carry it on to completion until the day of Christ Jesus.

Philippians 1:4–6

Who began the good work in us? God did.

And who is carrying on that good work in us, until it is complete? God is!

God allows these things—old shame on a bungee cord—to come bouncing back to us in his perfect timing.

Remember, there is an enemy who wants to steal, kill, and destroy; and as God increases our impact, influence, and fruitfulness, the enemy steps up his efforts to take us out. But God is never caught off guard! He reveals not-yet-fully-healed areas so we can be healed and whole for the next level of our calling, relationships, and purpose. This is great news—even if it does make us squirm a bit. You will be mature and complete, not lacking anything. God said so. He is at work completing you. When we understand that when we're being challenged emotionally or when someone hurts us, we have the opportunity to recognize our past broken responses and patterns, surrender to God's healing touch, and resolve to become shame-lifters rather than shame-makers.

Staying Free

So many believers make it this far: They decide to risk exposure and reach for healing from shame; they change their posture and start moving while still hurting; they make it through their exodus and even experience one or more sea-parting miracles; they get through the wilderness and step determinedly into their promised land—tearing down walls and facing their giants. Then they experience a bungee-cord moment. They see the baggage they are still dragging, *and they stop there!* Their eyes remain glued to the ugly baggage exposed—and all they can think about are all the shame-filled memories of the past.

Shame will always want to recapture you at that point and once again take you hostage. It will run wild with accusations if you allow it, pointing gleefully at every ugly piece of dirty laundry still packed in your baggage. It will work so hard to remind you how long you've been carrying it, and it will resort to its old lie: "You'll never be rid of it."

But as hard as it is at times, I'm determined I won't let bungee-cord shame take me out. I won't tuck tail and run. That is why I kept writing this book. I refused to quit writing a book on shame-free living just because my shame triggers were, well, triggered!

Let's face it, this side of heaven, we are still flawed and imperfect people, surrounded by flawed, imperfect people, all dealing with life in a broken, hurting world. Only by understanding how to apply the biblical principles that I've shared in this book will we continue to break the power of shame in our lives and be able to live the victorious Christian life. No matter the trigger, we must make what Jesus did for us bigger than what anyone has done or said to us.

God is at work transforming us into the kind of Jesus-followers who spread grace and appreciation and build up others in the Lord—a beautiful supernatural transformation! The next time someone hurts us—and they will—or we hurt someone—and we will—rather than *hide* from the pain and the shame, we can expose it to God's light and experience healing. This is living out grace. This is living in hope and promise rather than returning to the old cycle we dwelt in so long.

Let's see what God sees! Let's focus *on the freedom that is coming* once we drop our old baggage. Let's focus on where God is leading us. The next time all that bungee-cord shame comes flying back at you, take a moment to catch sight of the freedom to come when you slay that giant.

- Remember that God brought you to this moment on purpose, to prepare you for your future.
- Thank God for the challenge that exposed the giant.
- Declare your determination to follow, trust, and obey rather than running back to the wilderness to grumble and complain.
- Be confident that God will be faithful to lead you to complete freedom.

Freedom comes when we see ourselves as God sees us! For when we see the victory ahead, when we see the freedom that is coming, we not only are willing to endure, but are eager to press forward to pick up that freedom.

So on my knees, in a counselor's office, and with my accountability partners, I sought and invited God's transformation—as I had before. No doubt, as I will again someday. Immersed in God's Word, I focused on where he had set his sights to take me rather than on where my own warped shame lens told me I was stuck. I wasn't where I had started years ago—an epic control freak with trust issues—but I had residual effects of shame still shouting at me louder than I could shout back.

Once again, I worked hard to understand how parts of my broken past still lingered in my present, that I knew would impact how much of my promised land I would possess in the future. I dug into God's Word to learn how to measure my value and worth by the incalculable love of God. I prayed verses of confession. I memorized verses of forgiveness. I sought help tearing down walls. I refused the giant a victory. I sought the power of the Spirit to relinquish anger, not harbor bitterness or allow rejection to take root in my heart, and to choose to see others through the eyes of Jesus.

All at a deeper level.

And I watched God fight for me. Deliver me. And vindicate me. It wasn't about what had happened—being hurt; it was about my getting more and more free. It's an ongoing process, not a once-in-a-lifetime event but a journey. An adventure in freedom with God.

By defeating that giant, I experienced a new level of freedom. Even today, I'm always growing internally, always possessing more of my promised land. The reflection of the woman in the mirror who looks back at me is freer than she's ever been. I have been learning anew to see what God sees, to anticipate what God is doing. God already knew I was freedom-bound. He already saw me as I would be.

The free Christine has been helped, changed, restored, loved, and healed. And not only that, she is a woman of God who helps, rebuilds, restores, loves, heals, and leads others to freedom!

We are loved by a God who is taking us to freedom to set others free. God has been preparing me all along for that freedom. He is dedicated to continually growing me, strengthening me, equipping me, and empowering me for the future he had planned for me.

He did that for me, and he *continues* to do it for me. He does the same for you. *God is completing you in Christ. Pick up your freedom and run with it!*

Will you stumble as you run, and maybe fall? Will you face a giant or two along the way?

Yes, but that doesn't mean you aren't making progress. Just get up, dust yourself off, and keep running.

That's what I do. Sometimes, when I come across an old battered suitcase packed to overflowing with baggage, stashed away in some dark corner of my heart—and I'm challenged with pain, hurt, stress, fear—I say, bring it on. Let's open it up and bathe it in the light. When I feel fear and am tempted to please a person rather than obey God, or when I feel like I don't fit in and my mind races back to kindergarten, I press forward and expose it all to Jesus. I don't ever, ever want to go backward.

God, test my trust! Expose my weakness. Empower me to follow, trust, and obey so I may become more like Christ and infiltrate this world with your transforming power.

God has worked in my life just as he worked in the Israelites' lives: *"Little by little I will drive them out before you, until you have increased enough to take possession of the land"* (Exodus 23:30). Little by little. Remember, when the Israelites reached the Promised Land, even after the walls of Jericho fell down, there were more giants and people groups to overcome. We never stop fighting the good fight of faith; we simply become better equipped for victory.

Brené Brown famously calls this "shame resilience."[1] It's when you are able to successfully acknowledge shame and move through it—by maintaining your worthiness and authentic self, by talking to yourself like you're talking to someone you love, by reaching out to someone you trust, by telling about your shame because shame hates to be brought out into the open.

The resilience you develop by facing your giants—by exposing them—strengthens you to keep going. Today I can look back and see how far God has brought me. (Take note: My growth is still a work in progress! As already noted, growth this side of heaven goes on and on. And there is no shame in that!)

My wounded heart that once sought comfort and validation in busyness, accomplishment, achievement, and perfectionism is finding peace instead in God's accomplishments and his perfection.

My hands that once held so tightly to the reins of control are learning to loosen their death grip, and to guide more and control less.

The heart that was so full of fear, doubt, insecurity, low self-esteem, anger, bitterness, unforgiveness, and rejection is being softened. Many of its walls have been torn down, leaving more room inside for love, joy, peace, and patience.

I've been learning that I don't need to be on guard to defend myself. Rather, I can allow the Holy Spirit to become my defense mechanism, because only God can do the impossible and tear down walls. I've discovered that I was not created to bear shame, that Jesus bore it for me. I've been letting God rebuild my true identity according to the Word as his beloved daughter, precious and redeemed.

I know you want to be free. So be on the lookout for the next time a shame giant comes crashing back on you. If we do not utterly destroy them, they will destroy us. When they come, it will be a new opportunity to run into the arms of God rather than hide from him. A new opportunity to confess, repent, and receive the gift of forgiveness—or to extend it. A new opportunity to celebrate that you are loved inexhaustibly—and so is everyone else.

You have no reason to live in dread of shame anymore. Now you can live in hope, because your loving heavenly Father knows you falter, and he calls you to come running into his arms. You can be confident that he will make it right—that he can and will bring good things even out of your challenges and will complete his perfect work in you.

Like the children of Israel, we are well able to possess the land (Numbers 13:30) because the God on the inside of us is bigger than any shame giant that will ever attack us:

- The hurt from the aunt who thinks there's something wrong with you—just because you've not married;

- The rejection from your ex who walked out, saying you were just not right for him anymore;

- The disappointment every time your boss passes over you and selects someone else for a promotion;
- The insecurity that comes when people say you can't be a good mother and have a career too;
- The fear of launching your own business or stepping out into a new ministry.

Let's be the giant-slayers God made us to be. Because every time you slay one more giant, you claim more territory, you gain more ground—and you gain more and more freedom from the power of shame.

Chapter 11

YOUR NEW IMAGE

W hen I look in the mirror, I don't see who I once did. When I was shame-filled, I could barely look at myself. It was painful to see the image looking back. Now I can look without wincing. In fact, I might even give myself an occasional wink and a knowing smile. I know the miracles that God has done.

And when I catch my daughters Catherine and Sophia looking at themselves in the mirror as so many young girls do, I am amazed at how free and unself-conscious they are before their own image. It is beautiful to see that because of the constant affirmation they have had from their father, they don't carry the negative baggage to their mirror image that so many women do—that I did.

I am captivated by the ease with which they obviously delight in their own reflection. They approach the mirror unhindered and uninhibited because they know they are fully loved and valued, chosen and cherished. It is because they believe this in the very marrow of their bones that they are free to be themselves. It is truly a sight to behold.

It has taken me many more decades to arrive at that

same place, because I started at a much different place. My image was so marred by abuse, rejection, abandonment, and unworthiness that my lifelong struggle has been to discover who I am in Christ, and then own who I am—even when people, culture, tradition, religion, and my own brokenness kept trying to put me in a box and hide me.

For most of my life, I did not know I was listening to the voice of shame, or even that there was a voice I was listening to. But I'm no longer the woman hiding, no longer the woman avoiding the image in the mirror. Today I see through a new lens, my resurrection lens, the "who I am in Christ" lens.

The love of Jesus Christ has set me free.

I was able to write this book because I finally feel comfortable in my own skin. I spent most of my life wondering why I just could not be like everyone else—"normal," as my mom used to say. I've always felt that I've never quite fit in anywhere. But now that I'm free from so much, I realize it's because God made me the way he has, specifically to do what he has called me to do. I can even see how Jesus is using all the painful parts of my past to bring healing, hope, and life to people.

Through the work of A21, God has taken the shame I carried of abuse, adoption, and abandonment, and is redeeming it for women like Yun.

Through the initiative of Propel Women, God took the shame of all the leadership qualities the enemy tried to quench—starting in kindergarten—and is redeeming them to reach out to the many women struggling to manage life, leadership, and faith.

"God works all things together for good to those who love him and are called according to his purpose" (Romans 8:28, my paraphrase). I could not and would not be doing so much of what I am doing today if I had lived a different yesterday.

And I'm not the only one God has caused to triumph over shame. You've read the stories I mentioned throughout this book, some with more details than others. They are all women who are successfully learning how to trade shame-filled living for shame-free living . . .

Emma. Nearly ten years have passed since the day seven-year-old Emma, hiding behind the counselor's chair, began to break her silence concerning the shame she carried for the actions of her parents. As a teen now, she is still discovering that shame is a crafty adversary, reluctant to loosen its grip, crafty at crawling into our weakest places and waiting in silence only to rear its ugly head at our most vulnerable moments. But thanks to years of intentionally working to recognize shame, she has grown into a mature young woman with keen insights, determined not to allow the shames of her past to define her future.

Dianne. Never valued by her dad. Shamed in her job just because she was a woman. Now she is an amazing Bible teacher and speaker helping to set women free all over the world.

Yun. No longer a victim of human trafficking. No longer hiding behind every front. She's attending a university and building a new life, a beautiful example of the truth that no matter how painful or horrific one's past, Jesus can make all things new.

You. What would I have written about you? I'm sure you have a past, a story about shame, but it doesn't have to define your future. I hope you know that now.

My Dream for Every Woman, Everywhere

I want every woman, everywhere to live free from shame.

I want women who are trying to balance the demands of modern living, who carry so much guilt, who feel pulled in all directions, to live in peace and joy.

I want single women—and single-again women, either divorced or widowed—free from the shame of feeling "less than" because they aren't married.

I want women who are following their call and leading in all kinds of spheres to feel free to lead like who they really are.

I want stay-at-home mothers who feel called to serve there, but feel conflicted or condemned about not working outside their homes, to be proud of what they accomplish.

I want women who have failed to get back up again . . . no matter what knocked them down—an abortion, a divorce, an affair, a bankruptcy—to be free from shame.

I want women who cut, bruise, or burn themselves to be free from self-injuring triggers and the aftershocks of shame and guilt—and to find hope in Jesus.

I want women to know that the only image that will ultimately remain is the image of Christ within us. I want them to live free from the shame of not fitting society's perfect body image.

I want women who have been victims of violence or abuse to know there is always hope, and they can live again, truly live.

I want women who are lonely, isolated, and struggling to dare to come out of hiding and discover the power of love and community.

I want women who feel unloved and devalued to discover who they are in Christ and to be able to hold their heads up high and smile at the future.

I want women who live in torment, fear, and rejection to discover the healing power of Jesus and his unconditional love, grace, and mercy.

I want women around the world who are being violated, trafficked, burned alive, raped, and treated as less than human beings to be rescued and freed from the debilitating evil of shame.

I want women in war-ravaged countries who are running for their very lives, crossing borders to survive, searching to be reunited with their children and families, to find the miraculous power of our God and his will to free them from the inside out.

I want all women to dare to believe that God made them on purpose for a purpose. That he has filled them with gifts, talents, and abilities to be used to their full measure for his glory.

I want women to stop comparing and competing with each other and instead to love, support, and esteem each other as sisters in Christ.

I want women to know God can use everything the enemy meant for evil in their lives for good. He can take their stories of shame and redeem them—first for their own freedom and then to help others.

I want women to know that they are not less than, weaker, second, or not enough. They are created in God's image—greatly valued, loved, chosen, wanted, and adored by the Creator of the universe.

I want you to know that you matter very much to God.

God doesn't waste our hurts—not one of yours, and not one of mine. Looking back, I can see how God has taken everything in my past that the enemy meant for evil and he's turned it around. I think Joseph best summed up how I feel in Genesis 50:20, when he said to his brothers, *"You intended to harm me, but God intended it for good to accomplish what is now being done, the saving of many lives."*

It's Your Time to Shine

There is a work of the enemy to shame every woman everywhere—and it has gone on since the garden of Eden. Women around the world are being raped, beaten, abused, trafficked, murdered, burned alive, stoned . . . and that was just today's headlines. A hatred of women exists on this earth that is unbelievable, but God has a solution—you.

God is setting you free so you can go and free other women. He wants you to realize your potential—to put it all on the table unapologetically.

Your influence is not so small that you can't make a difference. God wants you to fulfill the purpose for which he created you. Jesus made you righteous; he placed his Spirit within you—and all his attributes. Yes, as you are transformed into the image of God, you become more like Christ, but really you become more of the "you" he made you to be.

So be her—and no one else.

Influence your world with your freedom.

I know you'll always be tempted to hide—especially the next time that bungee cord of shame comes your way. But you and I weren't created to hide. Quite the opposite. We were created to shine.

Jesus said, *"I am the light of the world"* (John 8:12). And later he said of us, *"You are the light of the world. A town built on a hill cannot be hidden. Neither do people light a lamp and put it under a bowl. Instead they put it on its stand, and it gives light to everyone in the house. In the same way, let your light shine before others"* (Matthew 5:14–16). Jesus wasn't contradicting himself but rather showing us the progression of how when his light floods our souls, and swallows up all the darkness of shame, then we too become the light of the world. His light illuminates our darkness, heals our wounds, and then shines through us to others.

Jesus wants to shine brightly through you.

Yet, as author Carey Scott poignantly reminds us in her book *Untangled*, "The Enemy targets our womanhood because he wants us to be ineffective. As women, we hold a great deal of power and persuasion. We are wives and moms, daughters and friends. We have jobs and run companies. We are so often the glue that holds relationships together. And if the Enemy can shake our confidence and make us second-guess our value, it can have ripple effects now and for generations."[1]

So, let's inspire our sisters and daughters, whether natural, adopted, or spiritual, to live in the fullness of God's promises.

Let's refuse to pass down any shame, guilt, and brokenness to them, something that they might "catch" from us or accept because we are their example. Let's live ourselves as we hope our daughters will live—because that's the shape of life they will emulate.

Let's ensure that they know and see God working through women.

Let's instill in them a sense of responsibility—that though they can't control what has happened to them, they can take leadership of their lives from the present forward. They can choose God's truths over the lies of the enemy, abide in his Word daily, and live free.

Let's tell them that their lives count before God, that they are full of tremendous potential.

Let's call them to be a force for good on the earth.

Let's walk alongside them and together be productive and fruitful for the glory of God.

Let's help them realize too much is at stake for them to live bound by shame.

When we recognize attitudes of despair and defeat and frustration, of unfulfilled longings to serve God more fully; when we see that they are not finding their own way, but rather meekly accepting the way pointed out to them by others; let *ours* be the voices they hear, shouting out in victory that God is calling them as his daughters to a new way, a higher way, for which he has uniquely prepared them.

Let's shout out that God sees them. That he knows and calls them by name. That he has empowered each of them for a future he envisioned for them alone.

Shame Off You!

All of our stories are really every woman's story. The details may be different. The degree of tragedy may fluctuate. But the feelings of shame are deeply imbedded. Sometimes we soar, sometimes we limp, but let's stick together on this journey and propel forward into freedom so others can be free. We are meant to live—truly live—unashamed of whom God made us to be—today.

Unshackled from our past.

Unleashed from hiding.

Unmasked in our vulnerability and transparency.

Unmistakably made unique in his image.

Unapologetic for being a woman.

Understandable in our choices.

Unbound by our wilderness.

Uncluttered in our hearts and souls.

Undistracted in our thoughts.

Unfazed by any wall.

Unwavering in the pursuit of our purpose.

Undaunted in the face of the giants.

Unstoppable in our journey from shame-filled living to shame-free living.

Undone by his love, grace, and mercy.

Unlimited in our potential.

Unflinching in our loyalty to Jesus.

Unreserved in our proclamation of the gospel.

Untameable and dangerous to the kingdom of darkness.

Undefeatable because of Jesus' victory.

The world says, "Shame on you."

I declare, "Shame off you!"

Now go.

Go in and possess your land.

Go live the one and only life you will ever have.

Go fulfill your God-given passion, purpose, and potential.

Go lead others to Christ—and to freedom.

Be you.

Uncovered.

Unafraid.

Unashamed.

ACKNOWLEDGMENTS

I feel like one of the most blessed women on the planet. I am surrounded by incredible people who inspire me, encourage me, support me, and believe in me. You would not be holding this book in your hands if it weren't for them.

To my husband: Nicholas Joseph. You love me unconditionally, support me unequivocally, and make me unreasonably happy. Thank you for not letting me give up and for bringing me copious cups of coffee during the writing process.

To my girls: Catherine Bobbie and Sophia Joyce. You are the delight of my life. You are a gift from heaven and a joy to parent. Thank you for going to the park a ridiculous number of times because Mummy was writing her book.

To our A21 team: Adrian, Alla, Amanda, Amanda-Paige, Amena, Anastasia, Anders, Andrew, Angelina, Anna, Anne, Annie, Aris, Arne, Asle, Bodil, Brianna, Brit, Brittny, Callie, Camilla, CaraLee, Carmel, Charlie, Chelsea, Cheyenne, Christian E., Christian V., Christina, Corina, Cornel, Daniel, Daniela, David, Derrick, Dorien, Elizabeth H., Elizabeth V., Emily, Engelbert, Eric, Erina,

Ester, Esther H., Esther V., Everett, Francois, Gaylia, Genique, Georgia, Gilbert, Gjermund, Grace, Hadassah, Hannah, Hanne-Kristin, Hazel, Helena, Inga, Ingrid, Jake, Jana, Jarred, Jeremy, JoAnna, Joella, Jonas, Jonathan, Joshua, Julee, Julia, Kalli, Katie F., Katie M., Katrina, Kayla, Kelly, Kelsy, Kine, Kristen, Kristiana, Kristin, Kyle, Kyra, Lars, Laura, Leah, Leigh, Lexi, Lilly, Linn, Louise, Lubka, Luke, Maarten, Malina, Maren, Maria, Mariah, Marina P., Marina N., Marta, Marte, Matunda, Melissa, Meredith, Mihail, Miranda, Monica, Monika, Natalie, Nick, Nickie, Nicole, Nid, Nina H., Nina N., Noi, Odette, Olivia, Phillip, Plamena, Racquel, Renate, Rene, Richard, Robin, Roland, Ruth, Ryley, Samantha, Sara, Sarah, Sarahi, Sarra, Sneji, Solfrid, Stefania, Stefka, Sudjai, Suwat, Tina, Triphena, Valya, Wendy, Wesley, Yana, Yulia, Zhenya, and Zlatka. Your passion, sacrifice, commitment, and loyalty always blow me away.

To our Propel Women team: Alli, Ashley, Barbara, Beth, Bianca, Katie, Natalie, and Stephanie. Your dedication to seeing women fulfill their purpose, passion, and potential is inspiring.

To our Zoe Church and Project Europe teams: Aleksandra, Andrea, Ani, Ania, Annie, Anu, Aris, Avi, Ben, Berdji, Borislava, Brenda, Courtney, Daniel D., Daniel K., Daphne, Didi, Dima, Dina, Emilka, Emma, Emo, Ewa, Ewelina, Gabrielle, George, Heather, Iskrena, Itzo, Jamie, Joachim, Julia, Karolina M., Karolina J., Kasia, Katie, Kinga, Kingsley, Kiro, Krista, Lukasz, Maciej, Maciek, Magdalena, Maja, Manuela, Maria, Marianna S., Marianna

C., Markus, Mateusz, Matt, Maya, Melissa, Michal, Miro, Monika, Nadia, Nathan, Niki, Nina, Noah, Olga M., Olga S., Pawel, Peter, Petia, Petya, Phil, Piotrek, Pola, Radi, Raff, Sasho, Simon, Simona, Smyrna, Stavros, Themis, Tony, Tsetso, Vasko, Ventsi, Vladi, and Witek. Your devoted focus in building the church and advancing the gospel is remarkable.

Elizabeth Prestwood: I literally could not have done this without you. Thank you for helping me to find my voice and hold on to it.

David and Cindy Lambert: You are both incredible and have helped me to shape and frame important parts of this book.

To the Zondervan team: This is our third book together, and it is an honor to work with you. Thank you Sandra Vander Zicht for your wisdom, insight, and attention to detail. Thank you David Morris for your amazing support and commitment to this project. Thank you Londa Alderink, Tom Dean, and the incredible marketing team for contributing strategy and brilliance—you are all awesome.

To my spiritual mother: Joyce Meyer. You have prayed for me, supported me, loved me, counseled me, corrected me, and carried me unconditionally for decades. I would not be here today without you. Thank you for everything. I love you heart and soul, always and forever.

To my friend: Beth Moore. You have been in my corner cheering me on from day one of this project. Your prayers, encouragement, wisdom, and comic relief were a gift. For such a time as this.

To my pastors: Brian and Bobbie Houston, and my Hillsong Church family. Thank you for loving me as I embarked on the journey from shame-filled living to shame-free living. I never would have made it without having a safe place to call home.

To my Savior, King, and Friend: Jesus Christ. The One who bore my shame. No words will ever convey my gratitude to you. We know where we have been together. There is no one like you. No one. You have my life for all of my life.

NOTES

Chapter 2: The Power of Shame

1. *New Bible Dictionary* (3rd ed.), eds. D. R. W. Wood, I. H. Marshall, A. R. Millard, J. I. Packer, D. J. Wiseman (Downers Grove, Ill.: InterVarsity Press, 1996).

2. Judith Stadtman Tucker, "Motherhood, Shame and Society," *The Mothers Movement Online*, http://www.mothersmovement.org/features/bbrown_int/bbrown_int_1.htm.

Chapter 3: Reaching for Freedom

1. Developed from a sermon preached by Rev. Lowell E. Grisham, Rector of St. Paul's Episcopal Church, Fayetteville, Arkansas, http://stpaulsfay.org/12-07-01TheBleedingWoman.pdf.

Chapter 4: Woman on Purpose

1. "Lives Together, Worlds Apart: Men and Women in a Time of Change," in *State of World Population 2000* (United Nations Population Fund, 2000). Retrieved October 9, 2015, from http://www.unfpa.org/sites/default/files/pub-pdf/swp2000_eng.pdf.

2. U.S. Department of State (2007). *Trafficking in Persons Report June 2007*. Retrieved from http://www.state.gov/documents/organization/82902.pdf.

3. United Nations Secretary-General's Campaign (2013), "A Promise Is a Promise," in *Unite to End Violence Against Women*. Retrieved October 9, 2015, from http://www.un.org/en/women/endviolence/pdf/apromiseisapromise.pdf.

4. UNFPA. (2000). "Lives Together, Worlds Apart: Men and Women in a Time of Change," in *State of World Population 2000*. Retrieved October 9, 2015, from http://www.unfpa.org/sites/default/files/pub-pdf/swp2000_eng.pdf.

Chapter 5: You Get to Choose

1. Some of these thoughts were adapted from Carey Scott's book *Untangled* (Grand Rapids: Revell, 2015), 194.

Chapter 6: The Beauty of the Wilderness

1. International Labour Organization (2002), "A Future Without Child Labour." Retrieved October 5, 2015, from http://www.ilo.org/ipecinfo/product/download .do?type=document&id=2427.

Chapter 9: Tear Down the Walls

1. David Noel Freedman, ed., *Anchor Bible Dictionary*, vol. 3 (New Haven, Conn.: Yale University Press, 1992), 723–740.

Chapter 10: The Bungee Cord of Shame

1. http://www.mothersmovement.org/features/ bbrown_int/bbrown_int_1htm.

Chapter 11: Your New Image

1. Carey Scott, *Untangled* (Grand Rapids: Revell, 2015), 55.

EVERY 30 SECONDS

somebody is forced into the
bondage of modern-day slavery.
We exist to change that.

Our goal for humanity is simple: Freedom.

Join us as we work to abolish injustice in the 21st century.

A21.org @A21 @A21 @A21

PROPEL WOMEN

PURPOSE

PASSION

POTENTIAL

For articles, videos and other free resources, visit
www.PropelWomen.org

Unashamed Video Curriculum

Drop the Baggage, Pick up Your Freedom, Fulfill Your Destiny

Christine Caine

In this five-session video Bible study, author and teacher Christine Caine weaves examples from her life with those of biblical characters who failed but overcame their shame to show how God heals us and redeems us. In her passionate style, she explains that if we want to change our futures, we have to believe God is bigger than our mistakes, our inadequacies, our pasts, and our limitations. We have to believe God created us for a unique purpose, has a specific plan for us, and has a powerful destiny he wants us to fulfill.

Session titles include:

- Session 1: Run, Don't Hide (Run to Jesus, Don't Hide from Jesus)
- Session 2: Today Is the Day (Shame Off You Today)
- Session 3: Possess Your Inheritance (You Must Go In and Take It)
- Session 4: God Never Wastes a Hurt (Our Scars Can Become a Sign of Victory, Not Shame)
- Session 5: Highly Unlikely (God Uses Ordinary People to Achieve Extraordinary Results)

The companion study guide (DVD sold separately) will lead you and your group deeper into the video content with guided session-by-session discussion questions, personal reflection questions, and between-sessions studies to enhance the group experience.

Undaunted

Daring to do what God calls you to do

Christine Caine

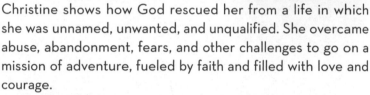

Christine Caine is no superhero. She's just like you. And she is changing the world.

Using her own dramatic life story, Christine shows how God rescued her from a life in which she was unnamed, unwanted, and unqualified. She overcame abuse, abandonment, fears, and other challenges to go on a mission of adventure, fueled by faith and filled with love and courage.

Christine offers life-transforming insights about not only how to overcome the trials, wrong turns, and often painful circumstances we all experience, but also how to grow from those experiences and be equipped and empowered to help others.

Her personal stories will inspire you to hear your own name called—just as Christine heard hers—to go into a dark and troubled world. Each of us possesses all it takes to bring hope, create change, and live completely for Christ.

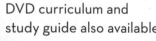

DVD curriculum and study guide also available

Available in stores and online!

Unstoppable

Running the Race You Were Born To Win

Christine Caine

Each of us has a race to run in life. But this is a different kind of race. It's more than a competition, greater than a sporting event. It's a race with eternal implications—a sprint to destiny.

But many times in our race, we're burdened and intimidated by life's challenges along the way. The task seems too tough, the path too perilous, the race too rigorous.

What if you knew the outcome of the race before it began? What if victory was promised before the starting gun ever sounded? This truth would change the way you live your life—revolutionize the way you run your race.

Slow out of the blocks? *It's okay. Don't give up!*

Trip and fall in the first turn? *Doesn't matter. The race isn't over!*

Disheartened by an unexpected obstacle? *Keep going. You can make it!*

In *Unstoppable*, bestselling author, global evangelist, and human-trafficking activist Christine Caine enthralls us with true stories and eternal principles that inspire us to run the race of our lives, receiving the baton of faith in sync with our team, the body of Christ.

Your race is now. This is your moment. When you run with God in his divine relay, you can't lose. You're running the race you were born to win. It's time to run a new way. It's time to realize ... you are unstoppable.

Living Life Undaunted

365 Readings and
Reflections from Christine
Caine

Christine Caine

You don't have to be a superhero to change the world. You just have to listen for God calling your name.

Drawing from her bestselling book *Undaunted*, as well as several of her other inspirational writings, author and advocate Christine Caine presents 365 thought-provoking devotionals that will inspire you to overcome your life circumstances, create change, and bring the hope of Christ to a dark and troubled world.

Each daily reading offers the wisdom, encouragement, and companionship you need to begin your own mission of adventure. Even if, like Christine, you began your story unnamed, unwanted, and unqualified, you can be fueled by an unstoppable faith and filled with Christ's relentless love and courage.

The world is waiting. Do you hear God calling your name?

Available in stores and online!